DOCTOR GEORGE'S MAGNIFICENT ZEPPELIN

DOCTOR GEORGE'S MAGNIFICENT ZEPPELIN

A Two Act Musical Play by

Grant Sutor Vuille

ISBN 978-1-257-93024-1

The Characters are Named & Dedicated
To the Memory of my Family Pets & to the Late,
Great, Musical Theatre Diva,
Ethel Merman

Character Descriptions

Doctor George

He is a middle-aged, or even older man who is a very kind, thoughtful individual. He is a genius of the fantastical sorts—an eccentric inventor bent on saving the world from evil, terrorism, and global conflict. Although he may say outrageous things, he always takes himself very seriously. He can often be a bit stuffy and bombastic, but remains a respected individual to his crew and surrounding characters.

Junie Moon

She is a young, glamorous TV reporter motivated to tagging along with, and reporting the great adventures of the famous Doctor George. She is an animated, involved, competent, and practical individual, and she is definitely not happy at all if she is not having her way. She knows when to put on the feminine charm to achieve her goals. Her presence helps to motivate the other characters into accepting new challenges.

Seymour

He is Doctor George's young male assistant and first mate and unrequited love interest to Junie Moon. He is awkward, yet dares to be fearless, but usually ends up cowering in fear. He is most attracted to Junie Moon, a person he immediately worships and reveres. Just glancing in her direction can be almost more than he can handle. When overcome by emotion or during sudden turns in the events and proceedings of the story he tends to lose control.

Max

He is Doctor George's young second mate and witty comic foil to Seymour and all the adventurous proceedings. Not too gullible, he is always amazed and frustrated by his ship mate's shenanigans. However, as naïve as Seymour might seem to him, he has genuine affection for him. Max is always able to come up with a witty remark to highlight the situation in which he and his colleagues find themselves.

Ethel, Buffy, & Gertrude Mermaid

They are the dazzling Mermaids of Mermaid's Isle who are colorful, animated, and very seductive characters. When they sing they light up the theatre with their vibrant, bold, performance, recalling the Andrew's Sisters singing in three-part-harmony. Ethel, the lead singer and the Mermaid's spokesperson, should be closely based on Broadway Diva, Ethel Merman—a brassy, vociferous, and in-charge individual whose clarion tone and timbre always dominates. Her equally colorful, glamorous onstage companions, Buffy and Gertrude Mermaid are also comic foils to one another in the same way as the zeppelin and pirate crew members.

Captain Bandit

He is a pirate captain who can be played as either a younger or somewhat older adult in the spirit of Captain Hook or Long John Silver. He is full of energy, dashing, handsome, and possesses a very robust, aggressive personality. As one of the antagonists he helps to get the story rolling with the adventure and eventual confrontation of the evil Fairie, Queen Thirteen. His antics help to create the tension and fun of the adventure.

Prince

He is Captain Bandit's rather astute first mate. Very bright and somewhat shy, he is often the one who seems to comprehend what's happening in the proceedings. He is Max's counterpart, and whenever onstage together, they can share an understanding. Their characters are simpatico.

Laddie

He is Captain Bandit's somewhat slower second mate. He can be as cowardly and fearful as Seymour, whose characteristics he resembles. He is always quick to douse his own fears by puffing up his chest and grumbling haplessly. He can frustrate Prince, and their comic foil personas mirror those of Max and Seymour, though their stations are reversed.

King Jaggar

As King of the Fairies on Jaggar's Isle, he can be played as a somewhat older male character, perhaps middle aged. He and Doctor George should share a positive space when relating to one another. He sparkles, glitters, and when not in his cage, he might be flying, dancing, and flittering about the stage. Being a Fairie, he could be small in stature, but since the actors themselves and their interpretations and characterizations of the Fairies are the most important factor, that isn't necessarily so. King Jaggar loves his wife, Queen Thirteen, but he is extremely intimidated by her.

Queen Thirteen

She is the evil, misguided Queen of the Fairies and wife to King Jaggar. She can be very imposing and threatening, elaborately coiffed, gowned in predominantly black, with hints of purple, orange, and yellow. She doesn't glitter like the other Fairies but often tosses about black, purple, orange, and yellow confetti—Halloween colors—to make a point or to emphasize a statement she makes. Her costume should have lots of flare, flash, be gnarly-looking and spiked somehow. She should be played with the authority of a wicked queen as she's the central antagonist of the story.

Fairies "Winkie, Dinkie, & Twinkie"

They are three cute little female/male Fairies who sparkle, dash, swish, prance, and spin about willy-nilly in close proximity to their leader King Jaggar. They are filled with comical mischief and lots of precocious bits of business. They sparkle, glitter, and prance about more so than their beloved leader, King Jaggar. They've got plenty of Fairie dust in their pockets to toss about, and they can even be given voices, such as squealing, giggling, and laughter in the absence of actual lines in the play. Whenever they 'speak' it is interpreted as Xylophoneze in which a Xylophone from the orchestra highlights their speech. When all the characters onstage sing in full chorus they can use their natural voices. However, their antics should not be so obtrusive as to distract from the other characters or the progression of the story.

Jumper the Dragon

Jumper is a high-spirited green dragon. A male actor of some stature could play him, dressed up in a colorful green dragon costume. He should be sassy and aggressive, and all the characters should respond completely horrified and intimidated at his presence. Underneath his green scales, Jumper the Dragon is a pussycat with a lot of warmth who dislikes his job as Queen Thirteen's primary henchman. He actually helps to unify the evil-versus-good characters of the play, with an uncanny interpretation of the whole adventure. Jumper the Dragon is an unwilling participant on the scene, and he is definitely over the whole situation, wanting just to go back to his cave, blow smoke rings, and rest.

OFF-STAGE CHARACTERS

Mr. Whopperberg

He is the W.H.O.P. TV Station Manager, a gruff, crusty character who is Junie Moon's boss. She makes calls to him on her cell phone and refers to him in the dialogue as the motivating force of getting her story told.

Gloria Glamorude

The hard-hitting reporter a la Barbara Walters who is extremely gossipy, rude, and whose mention of exposure to Doctor George's Vanity-Ego-Reflector as the play begins is the moment that sparks the stories and adventures for Junie Moon.

Act 1 – Scene 1

Doctor George's Home in the U.S.A.

Act 1 – Scene 2

The Skies on the Way to Adventure

Act 1 – Scene 3

Experiencing Mermaid's Isle & the Pirates

Act 1 – Scene 4

Off to Rescue Junie Moon

**** Intermission ****

Act 2 – Scene 1

Thirteenland & The Source of True Evil

Time

The time shall be a comfortable, fantasy-dream-land present day period, perhaps somewhere in the early 21st Century. There should always be a sense of reverence for the future. "Once upon a time" applies to this story.

Setting

Doctor George's home in the land of the free, the United States of America, the skies on the way to Mermaid's Isle, the pirate's oceanic domain, and the fabulous, exotic Isle of Jaggar (a.k.a. Jaggar's Isle) home to King Jaggar, his misguided want-to-be-evil-terrorist wife, Queen Thirteen, a plethora of mischievous Fairies, and Jumper the Dragon.

Act 1 – Scene 1

Doctor George's Home in the U.S.A.

(MUSICAL OVERTURE COMPLETES, LIGHTS UP as the CURTAIN OPENS revealing the large ZEPPELIN CENTER STAGE. There are a few SMALL LAND MASSES with SHRUBS and TREE PROPS on STATIONARY WAGONS completing the setting. DOCTOR GEORGE ENTERS STAGE LEFT and CROSSES to CENTER STAGE. He is a crusty, lovable, older gentleman dressed in a baggy, but colorful vested suit. He looks as though he would fit comfortably into a long ago century. His ZEPPELIN, a large, cucumber shaped BALLOON, nearly fills the UPSTAGE area. NETS and dozens of ROPES support the GONDOLA which resembles a small SPANISH GALLEON, its BOW pointing OFF STAGE LEFT, and with an UPPER PILOT'S DECK, STAGE RIGHT. This is where we have the CAPTAIN'S STEERING WHEEL, CONTROL LEVERS, FLASHING LIGHTS, ENGINE PROPELLERS, and SMOKING, SQUEAKING PIPES. DOCTOR GEORGE is followed on from STAGE LEFT by a beautiful young in-your-face TV reporter by the name of JUNIE MOON, who brings with her a small VIDEO CAMERA. SEYMOUR and MAX, DOCTOR GEORGE'S first and second crew mates, are on the ZEPPELIN, preparing for departure. They run about making adjustments to the ROPES, MECHANISMS, etc. They are DOCTOR GEORGE'S young dashing helpers and companions, who honor him with their respect and faithful servitude)

JUNIE MOON

(Aggressive, news reporter attitude)

Doctor George, can I please have a word with you before you depart? Can't you tell me anything about this mysterious journey you're about to take? The public has a right to know! As a citizen of United States of America, and as an attractive, glamorous, rookie TV newscaster, I demand you give me a statement!

DOCTOR GEORGE

(Polite, but sternly)

I'm sorry, Miss Moon, but if I were to reveal anything to you about this mission, then it would no longer be top secret! I am under a classified commission by the United States Government to carry out sensitive experiments. To tell you any more would undermine this entire enterprise. Is everything secure, Seymour? Max?

SEYMOUR

(Dashing about, doing bits of business)

Aye, aye, Doctor, she's ready to fly!

(Checking ENGINE PROPELLERS)

Propellers engaged and ready to crank!

(Goes to the ANCHOR)

Standing by to hoist anchor!

(MAX fiddles with DIALS and LEVERS, SMOKE and STEAM emits as CONTROL LIGHTS FLASH)

MAX

Propane heater units are fired up and ready to go, Doctor George! Ready when you two are!

DOCTOR GEORGE

(Delighted)

Excellent! Prepare to hoist anchor!

JUNIE MOON

Doctor George, don't you remember Gloria Glamorude, our gossip reporter from W.H.O.P. TV who came by to see you and got a glimpse at that secret device of yours? It totally transformed her from a rude reporter into a female version of Mr. Rogers! She said she'd smear you across the airwaves if you didn't disclose your vacation plans or your secret weapons device.

DOCTOR GEORGE

What? Oh, yes, that insolent Gloria Glamorude—she got a peek at my top secret invention, even though I tried to stop her! She threatened to expose me naked before the public conscience! Imagine that! I sent her packing!

JUNIE MOON

Yes, you did, indeed! And when she returned to W.H.O.P. TV she went on the air talking about hearts and flowers instead of her normal in-your-face newscaster attack persona.

DOCTOR GEORGE

(Smiling, reflecting)

Hmm...I doubt she will be bothersome to anyone ever again...ha, ha, ha...what a relief that will be for everyone in the TV news casting profession. Serves her right! She accused me of being a closeted bed-wetter! Ha, ha! Nosey reporters like you and she are everywhere on the TV and in-your-face, as you say. Ugh! Appalling! Gives me the shudders!

JUNIE MOON

I must insist that you allow me to travel with you. The public has a right to know, top secret or not! What did happen to my co-reporter Gloria Glamorude, Doctor George?

DOCTOR GEORGE

No, Miss Moon, no!

JUNIE MOON

She had accused you further of being up to dirty tricks, wire tapping, and even receiving hush money for your incredible invention!

DOCTOR GEORGE

Haven't you heard a thing I've said to you? I said, "No!"

JUNIE MOON

Later, that same evening, on the 7:00 p.m. newscast at W.H.O.P. TV, she had been transformed into a 1960's flower child! Her iconoclastic image as a hard-nosed-in-your-face-newswoman had been totally ruined!

DOCTOR GEORGE

(Annoyed)

Enough of this in-your-face bunk! Miss Moon, really, have you news people no scruples? If I were to reveal more than is generally known, then the safety of my dedicated crew and I would be in serious jeopardy.

(SEYMOUR and MAX show off for JUNIE MOON as she aims her VIDEO CAMERA at them. They make muscles and pose, etc.)

JUNIE MOON

Your crew members are quite entertaining.

(DOCTOR GEORGE glares at them and they return to duty)

Might I have a word with them?

DOCTOR GEORGE

Most emphatically not! Max! Seymour! Prepare for the ascent! The idea! Horsing around for the TV camera. To your posts! Miss Moon, do not attempt to board this vessel!

(DOCTOR GEORGE charges up the GANGPLANK CENTER STAGE and positions himself on the PILOT'S BRIDGE. MAX takes the CAPTAIN'S WHEEL as SEYMOUR loosens the MOORING ROPES. JUNIE MOON sneaks ONBOARD and approaches SEYMOUR near the GANGPLANK)

JUNIE MOON

Are you Mister Seymour?

SEYMOUR

(Impressed at being recognized by such a beauty)

Yes, Ma'am. Gosh, you sure are such a pretty lady! Am I going to be on TV? I've always wanted to be a TV person who's appearing with the beautifully rich and famous, celebrity TV people.

JUNIE MOON

Well, thank you for the compliment, Seymour. My name is Junie Moon. I'm a rookie TV newscaster intent on clawing my way to the top of the TV news business. And glamour does have its advantages.

(JUNIE MOON indicates the BEAUTY SPOT on her right cheek and bats her eyes at SEYMOUR seductively)

MAX

(Observing)

Behave yourself, Seymour

JUNIE MOON

I didn't earn this beauty spot on my cheek by schlepping around the TV studio getting hoots and whistles from the studio crew!

SEYMOUR

(Admiring the BEAUTY SPOT)

Hubba, hubba, girl, an actual beauty spot, just like Liz Taylor's! Now I'm twice as attracted to you as before!

JUNIE MOON

(Enjoying the compliment, demure)

Yes, yes, it's all a part of the game, sweetie—and it helps me get my stories when people are attracted to me.

(Calculating)

Yes, Seymour, dear, you will be on TV, but only if you can tell me about this mission of Doctor George's that's about to begin.

(Checking before speaking, SEYMOUR looks around secretively)

SEYMOUR

(Intimately)

Gee, uh…Junie Moon…I like your name—but Doctor George swore me to secrecy. I can tell you, however, that we are going to be traveling halfway around the world!

JUNIE MOON

You must be very brave.

SEYMOUR

(Blushing)

Oh, yes, ma'am, thank you ma'am—Miss—Ms. Junie Moon…On the Isle of Jaggar we hope to—oops—it just slipped out….

JUNIE MOON

(With VIDEO CAMERA poised and ready)

The Isle of Jaggar? Oh! You mean Jaggar's Isle! Uh huh, go on, you were saying?

SEYMOUR

(Feeling awkward, worried)

Golly, please don't tell anyone I told you where we're headed or Doctor George will skin me alive! See you later TV lady, Miss…Ms. Junie Moon. I wish we could take you with us but it's much too dangerous. Now get off our zeppelin because I have to hoist up the gangplank. Hurry, before Doctor George notices you!

(She charges quickly off the vessel, then boldly turns around at the bottom)

JUNIE MOON

I live for danger, Mr. Seymour!

(SEYMOUR has begun his readiness duties, pulling, and checking ROPES, etc. He ignores her and JUNIE MOON turns away from him in frustration)

DOCTOR GEORGE

Is everything secure, men?

JUNIE MOON

(Talking to herself)

I simply can't miss out on an opportunity to document this adventure. It could change the world, and there might even be a promotion in it for me! A stepping stone to superstardom!

(JUNIE MOON sneaks back ONBOARD before SEYMOUR has a chance to pull in the PLANK. She hides inside a large PICKLE BARREL, LEFT OF CENTER pulling it closed with a short ROPE attached to the underside of the LID. It is near some CRATES which the characters can leap upon from time to time in order to pontificate)

DOCTOR GEORGE

Seymour! Haven't you hoisted the anchor yet? Max and I are impatiently waiting!

(SEYMOUR pulls in the GANGPLANK)

SEYMOUR

Sorry, Sir, I'd forgotten to pull in the plank first—and then comes the anchor.

(Hoisting the ANCHOR)

I've got it now, Sir! Ready for lift-off!

MAX

(Amused)

You were flirting with that sexy TV reporter, Seymour. I saw you!

SEYMOUR

Shh! Mind your own business, Max!

DOCTOR GEORGE

(Miffed at their interest)

Oh, blast! I hope that nosy wench is gone! Has that rookie TV news gal departed?

SEYMOUR

I chased her away before I hoisted in the gangplank, Doctor George, Sir. Up, up, and away!

DOCTOR GEORGE

Excellent!

(He puts his finger to the wind)

The skies are clear, the wind's at our back. Let's have lift-off!

MAX

Aye, aye, Doctor George, Sir!

(MUSIC SWELLS as MAX and SEYMOUR throw SWITCHES, making CONTROL LIGHTS FLASH, SMOKE and STEAM BLOW, PROPELLERS SPIN, until off they go into the SKY via LIGHTING and DESCENDING PROP / PROJECTED CLOUD EFFECTS. The illusion of FORWARD MOVEMENT is helped when the few SMALL LAND MASSES with SHRUBS and TREES ROLL OFF STAGE RIGHT along with the CLOUDS. The OFF STAGE LEFT FAN can create the WIND EFFECTS when the ZEPPELIN is SAILING FORWARD THROUGH THE SKIES. LIGHTING EFFECTS and ACTION CONTINUE INTO ACT 1 – SCENE 2)

Act 1 – Scene 2

The Skies on the Way to Adventure

(MUSIC FADES. They are ALOFT. The OFF STAGE LEFT FAN continuously whips up a gentle BREEZE. A few BIRDS fly by on invisible wires DOWN STAGE LEFT to RIGHT. A STORK carrying a SWADDLED BABY from its beak also passes by. MAX is noticing these events)

MAX

(Mesmerized)

Look, Doctor George, someone's expecting!

DOCTOR GEORGE

(At the CAPTAIN'S WHEEL, he steps away to observe)

Ah, new life beginning. Isn't it exhilarating? Take the wheel, Max, we've reached cruising speed! Man the controls, Seymour!

SEYMOUR

(Taking MAX'S position at the CONTROLS)

Yes, Sir, thank you, Sir! Isn't the world beautiful from up above? It's so peaceful up here. I wish it were always that way on the ground. I wouldn't mind being a bird at all if I weren't so afraid of heights!

(He jumps back from the RAILING, fearfully, doing a double take)

Oh! It makes me dizzy looking down!

(DOCTOR GEORGE is at the BOW of the ZEPPELIN, scanning the earth below with his small TELESCOPE)

DOCTOR GEORGE

(Standing proudly)

It's the fear that men harbor which creates all the violence in the world. Only the quest for truth and knowledge can release mankind from his prison of ignorance. Face up to your fears, Seymour, and look down upon the Earth in its entire glorious splendor and you will soon be set free to explore the universe of the soul!

SEYMOUR

Oh, I'm okay as long as I don't hang over the side and look down.

(He peeks over the RAILING again)

Oh, what an incredible rush that is!

(He takes a few deep breaths and goes back to his CONTROLS and LEVERS)

I think I need a little break from that entire splendorous look over the side.

(He gets a little wobbly in the legs before righting himself)

Oh, help me.

MAX

You sure are a wise man, Doctor George, and you sure are a silly ass, Seymour! We've been flying this zeppelin for months! You should be over your fear of heights by now.

SEYMOUR

How do you conquer your fears, Doctor George?

DOCTOR GEORGE

(With exhilaration)

Take a deep breath. Look fear straight in the eye. Allow the universe to envelope you with the light and spirit of being. For it is at that very moment that anything and everything wonderful is possible!

(SEYMOUR, inspired, takes a few deep breaths and dashes towards the side RAILING, clutching it while looking down, but he suddenly faints and falls backwards to the deck with fear and trembling)

SEYMOUR

(Dizzy, rising to his feet)

Whew! I sure am glad I have this zeppelin deck beneath my feet! As long as we have it to keep us aloft, I'm not afraid anymore, I don't think.

(He grimaces)

DOCTOR GEORGE

(With warmth)

And, oh, what a Magnificent Zeppelin it is, too!

(The music begins for the song "DOCTOR GEORGE'S MAGNIFICENT ZEPPELIN" and DOCTOR GEORGE begins to sing)

I'm Doctor George and this is my Magnificent Zeppelin / We're sailing high, so high, up into the sky / With Seymour and Max along an adventure is imminent / So come along with us along with us and your spirit will fly / We will take her up and spin around, don't worry about a thing / With Seymour and Max right by our sides we then can really sing / I'm Doctor George and this is my Magnificent Zeppelin, so come along...

MAX & SEYMOUR

So come along…

DOCTOR GEORGE

So come along. We're flying high...

MAX & SEYMOUR

We're flying high...

DOCTOR GEORGE

So very high. So high, so high...

MAX & SEYMOUR

So high, so high...

DOCTOR GEORGE

So very high...

MAX & SEYMOUR

So very high...

DOCTOR GEORGE, MAX, & SEYMOUR

Up into the skies!

(Repeat from the beginning, MUSIC ONLY, as they DANCE and CAVORT about. JUNIE MOON slyly sneaks out from inside her PICKLE BARREL hideaway and begins VIDEOGRAPHING them awkwardly DANCING. MAX and SEYMOUR sing a SECOND VERSE, DANCING TOGETHER, as DOCTOR GEORGE claps his hands, standing aside, somewhat winded)

MAX & SEYMOUR

He's Doctor George and this is his Magnificent Zeppelin / He's flying high, so high, right clear through the skies / With us along we're sure to encounter adventures / So have no fears and soar with us through the air / We will fly about doing loop-de-loops, throwing away our cares / We're the greatest crew he's ever had and that is why we share / He's Doctor George and this is his Magnificent Zeppelin / So come along…

DOCTOR GEORGE

(Joining in the singing)

So come along...

MAX & SEYMOUR

So come along. We're flying high...

DOCTOR GEORGE

We're flying high...

MAX & SEYMOUR

So very high. So high, so high...

DOCTOR GEORGE

So high, so high...

MAX & SEYMOUR

So very high...

DOCTOR GEORGE

So very high...

DOCTOR GEORGE, MAX, & SEYMOUR

Up into the skies!

(JUNIE MOON dashes back and gets inside the PICKLE BARREL as SEYMOUR begins SWABBING the DECK with a MOP and BUCKET. JUNIE MOON peeks out at him from her hiding place. Each time he catches a glimpse of her, she ducks back inside the PICKLE BARREL. This little charade continues for a few short moments until SEYMOUR casually goes over to the PICKLE BARREL and lifts up the LID to peek inside. JUNIE MOON pokes her head up and he pretends not to notice her)

SEYMOUR

Yummy yum, yum, what tasty pickles have we here? Doctor George! Max?

(JUNIE MOON looks about desperately and then scrunches up even tighter so as not to be seen, though it is already too late. She continues poking her head out and peeking up at him from her hiding place while he catches glimpses of her. Finally, in desperation, JUNIE MOON places a PICKLE directly in his hand. SEYMOUR takes a bite, crunching it and enjoying the taste, then walks a few steps away from her)

Golly, these pickles are great! I could eat them all!

(He turns and winks at her, and startled, she ducks back inside the PICKLE BARREL again. SEYMOUR casually goes over to the PICKLE BARREL, lifts up the LID, exposing JUNIE MOON who peeks out at him looking worried, waving her hand for him to be quiet)

JUNIE MOON

Shh, please, Mr. Seymour, please don't tell Doctor George I sneaked on board—you'll give me away!

SEYMOUR

Ms. Moon, Doctor George can be very severe whenever anyone is caught spying on one of his secret missions.

JUNIE MOON

Please forgive me, Mr. Seymour, I know it was wrong of me, but I just couldn't miss out on an opportunity like this. You won't tell on me, will you?

SEYMOUR

But I must! It is my duty to inform him. I could be discharged for harboring a spy.

JUNIE MOON

But I'm not a spy! I'm a rookie documentary news reporter for W.H.O.P. TV on a very important assignment! Mr. Whopperberg, the station manager, sent me himself! Don't forget about my colleague Gloria Glamorude—Doctor George's invention transformed her—remember? She's sitting under a tree somewhere right now sucking daisies, thanks to him!

SEYMOUR

(Haughtily)

Ha! A likely story at best! How can I be certain that what you tell me is true? What proof can I have to verify this claim of yours?

(She holds up her VIDEO CAMERA. SEYMOUR adjusts his hair with spit in order to feel sexier)

JUNIE MOON

My expensive broadcast quality video camera, for one thing.

(She lifts the I.D. BADGE dangling from her neck)

Here's my W.H.O.P. TV I.D. badge, and--

(She reaches into a small SHOULDER BAG that she carries with her, pulling out a PACKET of PRESS PASSES and CREDIT CARDS)

--my credit cards and, most important, my many press-passes!

(They unfold before his eyes)

What more proof could you possibly need?

SEYMOUR

(Squinting, concentrating, examining the evidence)

Hmmm, I guess this proves you're not a foreign agent bent on the domination and destruction of the world as we know it—or does it? At least you seem to be from this country. You are a citizen of the Land-of-the-Free, aren't you?

JUNIE MOON

Of course I'm a citizen of the United States of America! Isn't it obvious? These half-dozen credit cards prove that alone! Americans are up to their eyebrows in debt!

SEYMOUR

(Nodding his head, thinking carefully)

Hmm, yes…the credit cards, naturally. That makes things clearer.

JUNIE MOON

(Relieved)

I take it this means you'll help me out and not toss me over the side wearing a parachute?

(Glancing over the railing, she gulps)

But to make things worse, we're flying over the ocean now!

SEYMOUR

(Hesitating, continuing to tease her)

Parachute? We only brought enough for three. I doubt if we could spare one as they're meant for us and our safety in an emergency. You'll just have to do without a parachute!

JUNIE MOON

Surely Doctor George wouldn't even consider such a barbaric act! I'll need a boat, too!

SEYMOUR

(Matter of fact)

And since we are over the ocean, you won't honestly need a parachute anyway, as you can just do a swan dive over the side and swim back to shore! One never knows about such things. When you're airborne, you have to obey the law of the skies.

JUNIE MOON

Which are?

SEYMOUR

(Shrugging)

Anything goes!

(Shocked, she throws her arms around him)

JUNIE MOON

Oh, Seymour, I beg of you, please don't turn me in to Doctor George, I'll do anything you ask of me! Besides, Mr. Seymour, I'm afraid of flying.

(She swoons, shuddering as she glances over the side again)

Oh! Ugh, and heights, and water! You, see, I fell off my grandfather's knee when I was a child….

(Dizzily, clutching him tightly)

Oh, I think I'm going to be sick!

SEYMOUR

(Thoughtfully)

This is certainly a coincidence.

JUNIE MOON

Are you going to be sick, too?

SEYMOUR

(Comforting)

No, nothing like that, Miss Moon, it's just that we both seem to have the same things in common.

(DOCTOR GEORGE has been on the BRIDGE, scanning the skies with his TELESCOPE. MAX controls the CAPTAIN'S WHEEL)

DOCTOR GEORGE

Clear skies ahead, by thunder! We're out over the seas on the way to Jaggar's Isle!

(Crossing to MAX)

Max! Give me the captain's wheel and fetch me a treat! I'm simply dying.

MAX

(Horrified)

Surely not, Sir! If you're ill, maybe we should call a doctor!

DOCTOR GEORGE

(Miffed, then more forcefully)

Dying for a little snack! Blast it all, Max, I'm not dying, you twit! I've a hankering for a fresh dill pickle! And I'll have you know that I am a doctor, so I know how to take care of myself, or my name isn't Doctor George, by thunder!

MAX

(Sheepishly)

I'm sorry, Sir, of course you're a doctor, Sir. By thunder it is, Sir.

DOCTOR GEORGE

And we don't have a telephone on board this vessel, so nobody's calling anyone. We haven't a radio or cell phone, either. You can't believe in them—our mission is top secret, and we cannot be sending out signals that might be picked up by the enemies of our great nation, which we are defending independently, and secretly, completely on our own—even the United States Government doesn't know the entirety of our plans! It is ours and ours alone--I'm speaking of our mission to save the world from evil, destruction, and all animal, vegetable, mineral, creature, being, and personal, catastrophic, environmental terrorism!

(He gasps)

MAX

Guess I forgot. Gee, Doctor, that was a mouthful—animal, vegetable, mineral, what?

(Scratching his head)

Um, gee, what was it again you wanted me to do, Sir?

DOCTOR GEORGE

It's time for a treat! Aren't you a wee bit hungry, too, Max, my boy?

MAX

Yes, Sir, indeed, Sir.

DOCTOR GEORGE

Good! Then won't you please be so kind as to allow me to take over the captain's wheel whilst you fetch us both a couple of fresh dill pickles from that pickle barrel over there?

(MAX salutes, standing at attention before springing to action)

MAX

Yes, Sir, your doctor-ness, Sir! Two dill pickles coming up!

(Hesitating, he dashes to the CONTROLS)

Just let me finish my adjustments and calculations for our propane hot air generator, first.

DOCTOR GEORGE

Blast it, Max, I can take care of that! Snap to it, my boy, I need that fresh dill pickle now! I'm famished!

(Nervously, reluctant to leave the CONTROLS, MAX shuffles back and forth with indecision)

MAX

But, Sir, it'll blow if I don't, uh, the hot air levels on these gizmos are dangerously high! And we don't know if she can take these pressures!

DOCTOR GEORGE

(Interrupting)

Don't be insolent, Max! I built all these controls and gizmo's and I know how they work! Bring me a pickle now and don't dilly-dally! I'm feeling faint and need a pickle to boost my metabolism posthaste!

MAX

Yes, Sir, yes, Sir, right away, Sir!

(MAX drops what he was trying to do with the CONTROLS and rushes to the PICKLE BARREL where JUNIE MOON has been hiding. DOCTOR GEORGE manages to bumble a bit and make a few awkward mistakes causing SMOKE and STEAM to emit. He reacts with alarm, jumping around while trying to steer the CAPTAIN'S WHEEL, which is difficult while adjusting the CONTROLS. As MAX approaches the PICKLE BARREL, SEYMOUR turns to JUNIE MOON who has been clandestinely watching the preceding's)

SEYMOUR

Quick! Get back inside the pickle barrel!

(She pulls the LID closed. SEYMOUR then whistles a tune, dusts with a RAG, adjusts ROPES carelessly, and finally has an awkward time with his MOP and BUCKET. All the while, MAX struggles to open the PICKLE BARREL, but JUNIE MOON keeps it shut by pulling on the ROPE inside. MAX'S struggle to open the PICKLE BARREL can trade off with SEYMOUR'S unsuccessful attempts with the various props)

MAX

(Frustrated, exhausted)

Seymour, will you help me with this confounded pickle barrel? The lid's stuck and I can't open it!

SEYMOUR

(Suddenly macho, forgetting about JUNIE MOON'S plight)

Stand aside, Max, and let a real man show you how it's done!

MAX

(Offended)

A real man? Are you insinuating that I'm not man enough for the job?

(SEYMOUR, wanting to impress JUNIE MOON, struts about puffing up his chest)

SEYMOUR

(Reflecting, self centered)

Not at all, my friend, but if you wanna impress the ladies, ya gotta show 'em a little beef, eh? Rise to the occasion, so to speak!

(SEYMOUR raises his eyebrows up and down with a confident smirk)

MAX

(Highly amused)

Oh, Seymour, come on, this is Max you're talking to, mate.

(SEYMOUR starts off with the OIL CAN, in which he generously lubricates the LID, but shooting and spilling some OIL over the side RAILING into the ocean. DOCTOR GEORGE witnesses this act and is alarmed)

DOCTOR GEORGE

Good, God, Seymour! Don't spill that filthy oil over the side into the ocean below!

SEYMOUR

But I was trying to—I needed to….

DOCTOR GEORGE

Don't you know that oil and water don't mix? Are you single handedly trying to destroy the ocean's environment?

SEYMOUR

Golly, Sir, I'm sorry! I don't want to disturb the sea creatures!

DOCTOR GEORGE

May I remind you, Seymour, my child, that this secret mission of ours is out to thwart terrorists! Including environmental terrorists!

SEYMOUR

Gee, I was just trying to get the lid off to get you a pickle. I'm not a child, Sir.

DOCTOR GEORGE

Selfish, inconsiderate, thoughtless deeds are the acts of children!

MAX

(Gloating, stifling laughter)

You're a man-child, Seymour, a terrorist man-child, ha, ha.

DOCTOR GEORGE

Enough nonsense! Return to your previous assignment to fetch me a pickle—but please, no more naughty pranks or mistakes!

MAX

You heard the good Doctor, Seymour.

(SEYMOUR mutters, puts the OIL CAN aside, and then tries every technique that MAX had tried but still fails to open the PICKLE BARREL. He begins speaking to JUNIE MOON in a harsh whisper)

SEYMOUR

Geez, Louise, you can let go, now. Miss Moon, it's just me, Seymour, your friend, remember?

(Chortling nervously)

She's tougher than I thought! Don't worry, guys, I can get it! She can't stop the courageous Seymour, manly man among men!

MAX

You mean, man-child among men, don't you?

DOCTOR GEORGE

Remember, Seymour, It's better to have tried and failed, than to have not tried at all.

MAX

(Heckling)

Failure is not an option, try, Seymour, try, lest you fail...psst, fail, fail you fool!

JUNIE MOON

(Whispering back desperately)

Psst! Seymour! Have you lost your mind? You'll give me away! I'm hiding here! I don't want to be thrown into the ocean without a parachute!

MAX

She? She, who? Are you talking to us, Seymour?

SEYMOUR

Did I say she? Just a figure of speech is all that is, Max. You know, just like the zeppelin. She's a great zeppelin, ain't she?

MAX

(Proudly admiring)

Yes, I see, Seymour. She's a great, magnificent zeppelin, isn't she, Seymour? What about dill pickle barrels, then?

SEYMOUR

Well….

(Indicating the PICKLE BARREL)

She's a great, magnificent dill pickle barrel, of course, Max!

MAX

(Shaking his head)

Yeah, I guess. If you say so.

SEYMOUR

Of course I say so. I wouldn't lie about a thing like that would I, Max?

MAX

(Shrugging, dryly sarcastic)

No, I guess not. But she's still not open!

SEYMOUR

(Imitating sarcasm)

Very well, then, I must say? Let's try her again, shall we, Max?

(Once again, SEYMOUR tries every trick in the book to try and get the PICKLE BARREL open. Then MAX tries to tug at it with him)

MAX

(Puzzled)

That's a mighty feisty pickle barrel. Let me try loosening the lid again, Seymour.

(Miffed)

If the pickle barrel's a she, then are the pickles inside of it all he's? Pickles are cucumbers after all, and their shape is--well, unusual, don't you think?

(MAX grabs at the HANDLE on the LID and tugs, but SEYMOUR pushes him away)

SEYMOUR

Not so fast, I can do it!

(Rubbing his hands together)

Guess I need a little elbow grease.

(He grabs the OIL CAN and oils the LID, then, rubbing his own elbows with oil, he begins speaking loudly to the BARREL)

Gee, I wonder if there are any dill pickles in you after all, Mr. Barrel, Sir. It'd sure be a shame if there weren't any, being as how we've all been working up quite an appetite trying to pull your lid off!

MAX

Pickle barrels can't talk, Seymour. Duh.

(SEYMOUR puts his arm around MAX, stepping away)

SEYMOUR

Max, you don't suppose Doctor George's enemies or a spy could have eaten all the delicious pickles inside this pickle barrel and have sealed it shut to protect the secret hiding place of the transmitting devices inside?

MAX

(Thoughtfully, distracted)

Spies? I seriously doubt that, Seymour. I don't think Doctor George has any enemies on board. We are off to Jaggar's Isle to fight the terrorist enemies of mankind, however—what are you getting at?

(JUNIE MOON pops open the LID with ease, handing SEYMOUR a big PICKLE. MAX doesn't see the exchange, but is suspicious when he notices SEYMOUR doing a double take)

SEYMOUR

(Fidgeting guiltily)

What? Oops! Oh, hmm. Silly me, uh, now, I'm going to, hmm….

(SEYMOUR steps quickly to the side concealing her as she pulls the LID shut. He grins sheepishly at the very suspicious MAX)

MAX

Are you up to something?

SEYMOUR

Here you are, Max, pal, a nice big salty green fresh one. I've never seen such a fat juicy dill pickle!

(MAX carefully inspects the PICKLE)

MAX

(Convinced of its authenticity)

Yes, indeed it is, Seymour. A delicious example from the deli in Pickle Heaven. I was wrong to doubt you. Thanks! Gee, it's large enough to make all the girls blush!

SEYMOUR

(Stifling gasp)

I don't think I know what you mean, Max.

(MAX takes his PICKLE to the BRIDGE, munching on it as he approaches DOCTOR GEORGE. SEYMOUR wipes the sweat from his brow and sits down on the RAILING, forgetting his fear of heights. He sighs with relief before recalling his fear and then leaps to the DECK. MAX is munching on his delicious PICKLE when he meets DOCTOR GEORGE who glares at him for forgetting to bring him one, too. MAX does an about face and returns to the BARREL for another PICKLE. JUNIE MOON lifts the LID open, just enough to extend her arm, and hands him another PICKLE to take to DOCTOR GEORGE. MAX takes it without thinking and starts back to the BRIDGE. He is halfway there when he suddenly reacts with a jolt, stops in his tracks, and stares at the big green DILL PICKLE in his hand)

MAX

(Puzzled)

Huh? Gosh! Did I see what I just saw?

(Rethinking carefully)

Amazing, prying open that lid was easier than I thought. I must have had an adrenaline rush of strength. Guess I'm quite the man after all, eh, Seymour? Run for cover, ladies, here I come!

(He climbs up the STEPS to the BRIDGE with speed, flexing his muscles. He hands DOCTOR GEORGE his PICKLE)

Here ya go, Doc. If you have other assignments requiring feats of strength, let me know!

(DOCTOR GEORGE nervously bumbles at the CONTROLS which are totally out of whack, SMOKING, WHISTLING, and POPPING)

DOCTOR GEORGE

Yes, you're back, thank Heaven, dear boy, I need you at the controls, now! I seem to be having a little trouble!

(Not yet comprehending the emergency situation, MAX continues to puff up and flex his muscles proudly)

MAX

Trouble? Yes, Sir, I know what you mean, Sir. Perhaps you noticed how I managed to open that pickle barrel singlehanded! I'm at your command, Doctor. What tasks have you to assign me with that will require a well toned individual such as me?

(He hands him the pickle)

That pickle barrel sure contains scrumptious treats within, it's a very friendly sort of barrel and I—huh? Wait a minute?

(Distracted from the emergency, DOCTOR GEORGE takes a bite of the PICKLE)

DOCTOR GEORGE

Delicious, this is a tasty treat, most definitely! Gentlemen, I have to agree with the both of you, she's a mighty generous pickle barrel to be sure!

MAX

Sir? I think maybe the barrel is alive!

DOCTOR GEORGE

Oh, how nice for the pickle barrel. Now, about these pressure gauges. I've been resetting some of them, and—

MAX

—Resetting? Oh, no, Sir!

DOCTOR GEORGE

Why, yes, I thought we needed more pressure and I—

MAX

--But, Sir!

(There is an EXPLOSION of SMOKE, STEAM, and FLASHING LIGHTS, all POPPING and CRACKLING at the SPUTTERING MECHANISMS and GIZMOS. They jump back at first and then try to regain control. JUNIE MOON pops out from inside the PICKLE BARREL, gets out of it and begins VIDEOGRAPHING the turmoil, while SEYMOUR rushes over to help DOCTOR GEORGE and MAX at the BRIDGE. To keep the excitement going the dialogue should be overlapping)

DOCTOR GEORGE

What, by thunder, have I done?

MAX

You busted a valve—get me a wrench, quick!

SEYMOUR

Merciful Heavens, the zeppelin will crash if we don't fix it!

DOCTOR GEORGE

Let me take the wheel!

MAX

Doctor George, help me with this valve, it's stuck!

SEYMOUR

Let me take the wheel, Doctor George, go and help Max with that stuck valve!

JUNIE MOON

That's it! That's what I like to see! Plenty of action! Max! Seymour! Show me what you've got! Doctor George, give me a nice profile, come on—puff out your chest, be daring--careful, not too much man-boob. Easy on the man-boob, Doctor George.

DOCTOR GEORGE

I'm not a man-boob, Seymour! Why do you insult me?

SEYMOUR

It wasn't me! I didn't refer to your boobs, Sir.

MAX

Help me tighten this valve, Doctor George, it's a tough one!

DOCTOR GEORGE

(Befuddled, near useless)

What? Did somebody else say something? Who's talking to me?

SEYMOUR

Max, hurry up, tighten that valve and reset the gauges or we'll lose all the hot air pressure and our zeppelin will crash!

(Moving around skillfully, positioning herself for better coverage, JUNIE MOON continues to VIDEOGRAPH the excitement)

JUNIE MOON

This'll be the big news item of the week! Flex those biceps, boys!

MAX

(Urgently)

Doctor George, I'm talking to you. Help me, please—grab hold of the wrench!

SEYMOUR

(Getting really panicky)

We're losing altitude! I want my Mama! I'm sorry I wouldn't eat my spinach, Mama!

JUNIE MOON

(Jockeying for position)

Stand aside, Seymour, I need to get a tighter shot of Doctor George!

SEYMOUR

(Freaking out)

Can you ever forgive me, Mama? I tried, Mama, Oh, how I tried!

DOCTOR GEORGE

(Gathering courage)

Never fear, Max! I have everything under control! Am I hearing voices? Tighter shot of what?

JUNIE MOON

Suck in that gut and show me some pecks, Doctor George!

DOCTOR GEORGE

Pecks? Some pecks? A peck of what, Max?

JUNIE MOON

Now you're kicking it up a notch! Hey, Doc, does this accident mean the mission will have to be aborted?

(Racing around, totally unnerved, SEYMOUR fruitlessly tries to pull it together)

SEYMOUR

Guys, hurry up and fix this thing, or we're all doomed!

(MAX'S confidence helps begin to calm the MECHANISMS)

MAX

I think I've almost got it! Stand aside, Doctor George! Let me do it!

JUNIE MOON

Doctor George, do your crew members have a health plan, or carry life and casualty insurance?

DOCTOR GEORGE

(Befuddled, confused)

Max, did you say something to me? I swear I'm hearing voices!

JUNIE MOON

(Aggressively)

In the event there are any survivors, Doctor George, do you expect them to sue you for damages?

(Focusing her VIDEO CAMERA for a close-up)

SEYMOUR

(Resigned, hands positioned in prayer)

Dear God, I know I haven't always been a good boy, but if you could find it in your heart to forgive me for not eating my spinach as a child, I know it would make Mama very happy. And I just want to say, I'd like to reside on a cloud in Heaven that's not quite as high as we are now.

DOCTOR GEORGE

I must be losing my mind. Yes, yes, by God, we have insurance!

MAX

Just a few more twists, Doctor George, and we're home free.

(Still breathing heavily, puzzling the situation, SEYMOUR, too, realizes that things are coming under control)

SEYMOUR

Hey, Max, good—boy, I think we've passed the danger point, she's coming around.

JUNIE MOON

Doctor George, can we now safely assume that the mission will continue as originally planned?

DOCTOR GEORGE

Yes, yes, I think we've recovered from our little mishap, eh boys? And of course we plan to—young lady, how did you manage to get on board?

(SEYMOUR goes to her side and puts his arm around her)

MAX

(Shocked)

Sir, there's a female onboard!

DOCTOR GEORGE

Quite so!

SEYMOUR

Please, sir, it was my own doing. I allowed her to sneak on board. I hid her inside the pickle barrel.

MAX

(Dryly sarcastically)

Ah, the mysterious pickle barrel gag! Now I get it! Very clever, Seymour.

SEYMOUR

You couldn't have done it without me, Max, so button up, there's a lady present.

JUNIE MOON

(Pleading)

I beg you, dear Doctor, do not throw me over the side. Have mercy, please, my intentions are entirely honorable. If Mr. Whopperberg at W.H.O.P. TV allows me to sell my video to the networks I'll give you a fifty percent split! We stand to rake in a generous amount of money which can easily help offset the cost of this secret mission of yours.

MAX

Hooray! Now I can afford to go back to college and become what I was meant to be!

SEYMOUR

Which is?

MAX

A rocket scientist! Zeppelins are so passé. They went out with the Hindenburg. Poof!

(Indicating an explosion)

I need a challenge.

DOCTOR GEORGE

Your offer is most generous, Miss Moon, but never mind about that just now, we'll discuss the details later.

(During this speech, SEYMOUR and MAX are quietly strutting, puffing up their chests, behaving possessively, and giving each other looks as if to say, lay off JUNIE MOON, she's mine)

JUNIE MOON

Look at your crew, Doctor, they want me to come along.

DOCTOR GEORGE

Boys, cut it out! We've not time to turn back, young lady, and you are a pest--I probably should throw you overboard!

SEYMOUR

(Shocked)

No, dear Doctor, no!

MAX

Gee, that's really harsh, even for you, Doctor George.

JUNIE MOON

Surely you must be reasonable, Doctor! It would be horrible to toss me over the side. If I drowned it would be murder!

SEYMOUR

(Begging)

Doctor George, no, no, you can't mean this—please spare her life!

MAX

(Assessing the situation)

Seymour may be right, Doctor. Murdering someone goes against all your mission's principles. We don't want to kill disagreeable persons, just reform them peacefully, don't we?

SEYMOUR

Listen to Max, Doctor George, Ms. Moon is not an evil person, or even a terrorist for that matter!

JUNIE MOON

Honestly, Doctor George, I only want to help your mission by documenting it. It's a golden opportunity to raise awareness for conflicts all over the world. Have mercy on me, dear Doctor, please!

DOCTOR GEORGE

Blast! You reporters are all alike! You make sense out of nonsense!

JUNIE MOON

(Meekly)

Just think how great it would be to have our own TV Special of the Week.

DOCTOR GEORGE

Like on PBS?

(Grumbling)

Oh, you mean that horrible Whopperberg channel, hmm, bah!

SEYMOUR

Mercy, Doctor, please, mercy.

DOCTOR GEORGE

(Shaking his head)

It goes against my civilized nature to be deliberately cruel.

(He grimaces at JUNIE MOON)

You may continue to document this mission.

SEYMOUR

Hooray! We'll be famous!

MAX

We'll be stars! Junie Moon and I, together at last!

SEYMOUR

Junie Moon, my sweet, I know you and I will last forever!

MAX

Come with me, Miss Moon, let us run off to the Casbar, together!

(They make a grab for her and clutch JUNIE MOON possessively, both attempting to pull her aside)

SEYMOUR

I got first dibs! I saw her first!

MAX

That's not fair! You're older, Seymour! Why don't you let us little guys with enough brains to go to college have a chance?

(Breaking free of both of them)

JUNIE MOON

Sorry to disappoint you boys, but I have other plans. There's an important mission here to document on video and that comes first. Doctor George, for starters, exactly where are we headed, sir?

DOCTOR GEORGE

To the ancient Isle of Jaggar, Land of the Fairies, to test out my secret invention which I hope will save the world from the evils of terrorism, fascism, and environmental abuses including all intolerable animal, vegetable, and mineral rights abuses. And of course, let us not forget, we will thwart the total spiritual destruction and annihilation of our planets citizens!

JUNIE MOON

How ambitious! What kind of invention is it, Doctor?

DOCTOR GEORGE

It's a special computerized mirror I call the Vanity-Ego-Reflector. Anyone who stares into its depths sees themselves exactly as they are—unmasked and naked before the universe. It's digital!

(MAX and SEYMOUR gush with excitement)

SEYMOUR

Digital?

MAX

Yes, digital.

SEYMOUR

Really? Super dooper electronic!

MAX

Magnetic, and radioactive, Doctor George?

SEYMOUR

How fabulous! Wow! I get it!

JUNIE MOON

(Skeptical)

Digital? I didn't think you were interested in digital things, Doctor George. You don't even have a cell phone!

(JUNIE MOON whips out her CELL PHONE to make a call)

Excuse me, Doctor George, I need to make a call to Mr. Whopperberg, the station manager at W.H.O.P. TV. I need to let him know our plans.

DOCTOR GEORGE

(Interrupting)

Don't make that call, Ms. Moon. Throw it over the side, quickly--we need to have our plans remain secret!

(JUNIE MOON thinks about this, hesitates, then fakes throwing it over the side, secretly tucking it back into her pocket)

JUNIE MOON

No more cell phone, Doctor. Gone! All gone, see?

(She shows her empty hands to everyone and smiles boldly. Satisfied that the cell phone is no more, DOCTOR GEORGE begins to explain his invention to them)

DOCTOR GEORGE

Digital? Twits! It's what all modern inventions use! If it's digital, then it has to be great! And all of my inventions are great!

(JUNIE MOON, SEYMOUR, and MAX gasp with incredulity. DOCTOR GEORGE shrugs and continues speaking to them almost reluctantly and matter-of-factly)

Corrupt and evil beings, and terrorist type persons, are instantly humbled when they see themselves as they truly are deep inside themselves! Don't forget about your gossipy reporter at W.H.O.P. TV —Ms. Gloria Glamorude—she will be rude no more! Ha, ha!

(Growing confident in his explanation of goals for the invention)

Gazing into it, sinister beings at once recognize the need to change their evil ways for a healthy, happy, compassionate, and peaceful lifestyle. Imagine living without prejudice, in complete harmony, peace, and alignment with all the living beings and fantasy creatures of the Earth! The world will become a paradise, a Heaven-on-Earth, as it were.

(He looks about mystically)

Of, course, as a Heaven concept, then somehow your favorite deity will have to be included, because we don't wish to exclude any spiritual quest others may wish to ponder. Yes, the Heavens are full of deities.

JUNIE MOON

Okay, doc, I got you. It's digital, yes, but what's its source of power? Deities in Heaven, or does it come with batteries?

DOCTOR GEORGE

(Gravely)

The source of its power is dark matter. Yes, indeed, the very substance that holds the universe together, by thunder! I'm the first inventor ever to harness its energy!

JUNIE MOON

Dark matter? Oh, yes, the thing astronomers, scientists, and physics professors contemplate.

SEYMOUR

I might like to work as a scientist someday. Will I need schooling, or can I just learn it on my own, like you, Doctor George? Where did you get your scientific ideas from, anyway?

DOCTOR GEORGE

From years, upon years, of personal sacrifice and study, Seymour, don't be insolent.

SEYMOUR

Forgive me, Sir, but honestly, where did you get all these wacky ideas?

DOCTOR GEORGE

Wacky? Coming from you, I'm sure that seems sensible. For your information, Seymour, I attended many, many universities and colleges for many, many years. My knowledge led me to the creation of my invention to save the world from evil.

JUNIE MOON

Great! That wacky invention ought to be a big seller among the politicians, the military industrial complex, and the soldiers everywhere fighting the evils of terrorists wreaking pointless havoc worldwide—that's genius, Doctor!

MAX

What will our religious leaders think, Doctor George? People of all nations worship so many deity varieties. Most don't like a scientific approach to conflict, especially the conflicts each of us have within ourselves.

DOCTOR GEORGE

Yes, Max, that is correct. And that's the secret of dark matter. It dwells within the entire universe, and it dwells within our very soul.

MAX

Jesus Christ said that Heaven is within. Was he speaking about Heaven being where this dark matter exists?

DOCTOR GEORGE

In my opinion, yes, but the secrets of dark matter are still just that; secrets.

JUNIE MOON

Keep talking, Doc, and you'll beat them all with the power of dark matter! Their evil minds will be reversed forever. Sensational!

SEYMOUR

Deity? What's that?

MAX

Gee whiz, Seymour—The Man upstairs—I give up!

SEYMOUR

Upstairs?

(Ignoring his crew's remarks, he continues)

DOCTOR GEORGE

Precisely, Miss Moon, with dark matter powering my device, terrorists, dictators, fascists, sociopaths, and criminals whose egotistical ineptitudes always result in revolutions, war, and violence, will be humbled, rest assured!

(CANNON FIRE, FLAMES and SMOKE shoots forth loudly as a prop CANNON BALL ENTERS STAGE LEFT and sails through the air, tearing through the ZEPPELIN'S BALLOON, leaving a LARGE HOLE. DOCTOR GEORGE grabs his TELESCOPE)

MAX

Doctor George, someone has shot a hole in the zeppelin! What shall we do?

DOCTOR GEORGE

Oh, my stars! Just as I thought! We've been cruising so low over the ocean because of our mishap that Captain Bandit the pirate has managed to hit us with cannon fire! Max, stay at the wheel while Seymour climbs up the ropes to sew up the tear!

SEYMOUR

(Frightened)

But, Doctor George, sir, please, no! I can't, I'm scared of heights, Remember?

(He hyperventilates)

JUNIE MOON

Seymour, you must, or we'll crash into the sea!

DOCTOR GEORGE

Quick, Max, hand me my Hypnotic Umbrella!

(MAX gets it from one of the CRATES, hands it to him, and DOCTOR GEORGE opens it. It has a SPIRAL painted on it, and he spins it around and around, aimed directly at SEYMOUR, He spins it continuously throughout the scene)

MAX

(Skeptical)

Hmm, can this really work, Doctor?

DOCTOR GEORGE

Yes, Max. Never doubt me. Seymour! Listen to my commands! You are in a deep, deep trance. You are no longer afraid of heights! Believe in yourself, Seymour. Look deeply into the spiraling umbrella and concentrate. You can save us all my making the necessary zeppelin tear repairs.

(SEYMOUR reacts zombie-like and grabs a large NEEDLE and some STRING which he places in his mouth before he climbs the ROPES to the torn ZEPPELIN BALLOON. He is somewhat awkward and loses his grip a few times, startling EVERYONE)

JUNIE MOON

My goodness, you've hypnotized him. This is great stuff for my video.

(SEYMOUR begins sewing up the TEAR while EVERYONE cheers him on)

MAX

He won't hurt himself will he, Doctor?

JUNIE MOON

If he could only stay hypnotized he'd never have to worry about heights again.

MAX

Look at him, he hasn't flinched, he's still concentrating, that's a first!

JUNIE MOON

That's it! You can do it, Seymour! He's so brave, it's fascinating, a mouse becomes a man!

MAX

Ha! More like a mouse becomes a rat. No offense, Seymour, pal.

DOCTOR GEORGE

Continue with the necessary repairs, Seymour. Focus on how this is the easiest job you've ever had. You have all the necessary confidence to complete the task.

JUNIE MOON

This video is going to make history—give us more attitude, Seymour! Make us believe in you!

DOCTOR GEORGE

My hypnotic commands have successfully helped you in overcoming your unnatural fear of heights.

MAX

Wow, that a boy, Seymour! Gee, I guess I underestimated him. Doctor George, you amaze me. Can I borrow that Hypnotic Umbrella so I can pass my college entrance exams? I always get nervous and freeze up when I take tests.

JUNIE MOON

You're the man, Seymour, keep it up, play to the camera, the camera loves you! Show the camera you love it!

(SEYMOUR finishes the task and begins to climb down)

DOCTOR GEORGE

Gaze deeply into the Hypnotic Umbrella, you will return to normal when I stop spinning it.

MAX

Uh, oh, we're losing altitude again! We're going to have to land in the water!

JUNIE MOON

Give me a little profile, Seymour. I'm going to give you a special spot in our documentary.

MAX

It's a good thing this zeppelin gondola is able to float! I hope those pirates don't catch up to us, or they'll blow us all to kingdom come!

(Max takes over the controls)

We've lost too much hot air, Doctor George, I'm setting her down! Everyone, brace yourselves!

(AIR, SEA, SOUND, and LIGHTING EFFECTS begin as ACTION CONTINUES INTO ACT 1 – SCENE 3)

ACT 1 – SCENE 3

Experiencing Mermaid's Isle & the Pirates

(The ACTION CONTINUES as SEYMOUR rejoins them on the DECK. They set the GONDOLA down into the WATER. JIG-SAW WAVES on EITHER SIDE and IN FRONT of the ZEPPELIN ENTER from the WINGS and rock back and forth to allow it to appear that the ZEPPLELIN has landed in the ocean. DOCTOR GEORGE puts away the HYPNOTIC UMBRELLA as SEYMOUR comes out of his trance and leaps with fright into JUNIE MOON'S arms)

JUNIE MOON

Settle down, Seymour, you did a great job of repairing the balloon, we're all so proud of you.

SEYMOUR

You mean that?

JUNIE MOON

Sure I do, and I've got it all on video to prove it!

SEYMOUR

(Sheepishly)

Does this mean we can go steady?

(He embraces her, obsessing upon her mole)

Your beauty spot makes me want to love you all the more!

JUNIE MOON

(Releasing herself from his embrace)

Beauty spot? Silly, I paint that on! Liz Taylor was born with hers. It's simply not real, Seymour.

SEYMOUR

You paint on a replica of Elizabeth Taylor's beauty spot? Yes, Elizabeth Taylor's the movie star you remind me of--at least, the beauty spot on your right cheek does.

(Again he pulls JUNIE MOON closer to him)

Elizabeth was awesome on the movie screen back in the twentieth century—and you've got me feeling really warm and fuzzy inside! Perhaps I'm Richard Burton reincarnated, hubba, hubba, hubba.

(She squirms inside his embrace and begins pushing him back away from her, rejecting his attentions)

JUNIE MOON

Not so fast, Seymour. You're cute, but you're no Richard Burton, and I'm not sure you're even my type—you're too skittish! I need a man who is not afraid to stand up to me; you know, sweep me off my feet and run away with me!

(The PIRATE BOAT ENTERS from STAGE LEFT. It is a CUT-OUT PROP supported by the three PIRATES and it CROSSES TO CENTER STAGE quickly, then PAUSES as CAPTAIN BANDIT sweeps

JUNIE MOON OFF of the GONDOLA, continuing OFF STAGE RIGHT as she screams. The dialogue is under the action of her kidnapping)

CAPTAIN BANDIT

Shiver me timbers, you'll be coming with us, you sky wench, welcome aboard!

LADDIE

Oh, boy, Captain Bandit, are we kidnapping a beautiful angel? Prince, look!

PRINCE

Yes, Laddie, we'll be ransoming her for treasure! You belong to our domain now, lady; you're a sea pirates' delight.

JUNIE MOON

Help! Help! I'm being kidnapped by vicious pirates! Seymour! Doctor George! Max! Come and rescue me! Help!

SEYMOUR

Oh my goodness! Captain Bandit and his pirates have kidnapped my precious honey-bunch! Whatever shall we do?

DOCTOR GEORGE

We'll follow them closely, and then at exactly the right moment, just in the nick of time, we'll snatch her up and run away like crazy on our twinkle toes in the opposite direction!

SEYMOUR

Yeah, Doctor George, that's a great plan! You truly are a genius!

MAX

Twinkle toes? Impossible! We can't outrun vicious pirates! They'll capture us all and make us walk the plank, for pity's sake.

SEYMOUR

You're such a pessimist, Max.

DOCTOR GEORGE

I was speaking metaphorically. Naturally, we'll not have to run—this is not a track and field exercise—we'll just sail away up into the skies on my Magnificent Zeppelin, silly boys!

MAX

(Testy, losing patience)

Oh, fine, except that we're grounded—over water! And I hope we're not going to sink! Don't forget the ocean is underneath us, and the pirates have abducted our TV reporter stowaway, Junie Moon! Now, who will document our secret mission? We didn't think to bring a video camera ourselves, now did we?

SEYMOUR

Oh, no! This is terrible, Max! Are you saying our zeppelin won't fly?

MAX

Well, Seymour, I have to make some repairs first, and that'll take time. Meanwhile, the pirates are way ahead of us.

SEYMOUR

Why can't we just sail after them in the ocean? The gondola seems to float just fine. It's designed like an old Spanish galleon, and they're practically unsinkable—Captain Hook sailed around in one chasing after Peter Pan, remember?

MAX

Yes, Seymour, and the Crocodile still had him for dinner—well, perhaps she is sea worthy after all. The hole from that pirate cannon ball ripped through the balloon and not the gondola, thank goodness.

SEYMOUR

(Contemplating their situation)

Let's just say she drifts along. She's not as fast in the water as she is in the air, however, and our pirate enemies are making pretty good time in that speedboat of theirs.

MAX

(Admiring the ZEPPELIN*)*

Yes, this zeppelin definitely reminds me of those slow lumbering Spanish galleons from centuries ago—did you know Christopher Columbus, Doctor George?

DOCTOR GEORGE

Yes, of course I know who Christopher Columbus—was—I never met him, silly, you young people think anyone over thirty is ancient. Well, let's not be down hearted, I'll think of something. Get busy, Max! Make your repairs and stop flapping your jaw, while I scan the horizons!

MAX

Sorry, Doc, you know what's best.

*(*DOCTOR GEORGE *looks through his* TELESCOPE*)*

DOCTOR GEORGE

Blast, I've lost all sight of them! Without knowing their direction our search could take months!

SEYMOUR

(Aghast)

Months? My precious Junie Moon is lost to me forever! Whatever shall we do?

DOCTOR GEORGE

Seymour, stop belly-aching and help Max! The sooner we're aloft again the better I'll be able to see the pirates in my telescope and go after them! Perhaps I'll be lucky enough to spot them after all.

MAX

Come on, Seymour, let's get to work and get this Magnificent Zeppelin off the ground!

SEYMOUR

(Seymour shivers, arms folded across his chest)

Yes, let's hurry. We've just got to save Junie Moon! After all, it was love at first sight between us, you know—I could feel it in my bones!

MAX

(Sarcastically)

Yes, Seymour, yes, I'm sure. Hmm, that Junie Moon, I'll admit, she's a looker.

(MAX continues tinkering with the PIPE MECHANISMS with SEYMOUR'S help. SMOKE and STEAM is still leaking out from the damaged ZEPPELIN'S HOT-AIR-LIFT-ENGINE)

SEYMOUR

I think there's something wrong with these pipes, Max.

MAX

Darn! It's just as I was afraid of, Doctor George. The seal in this main valve has worn out, and I've nothing to replace it with!

SEYMOUR

You mean we can't fix the problem?

MAX

Unless this leak is repaired, we'll have no hot air pressure and the zeppelin will stay grounded—hmm--well, afloat.

DOCTOR GEORGE

Blast! That does sound serious!

(Spotting something though his TELESCOPE)

Wait a minute! I think I see something! Why, yes, it's the Mermaids of Mermaid's Isle!

(Excited, he begins to sound hopeful)

And they're singing us a song! The lead singer with the red bouffant hairdo is Ethel Mermaid herself, and her backup singers, Buffy and Gertrude Mermaid, are accompanying her with their lovely 'Siren's Song!'

(Turning to the CREW with great enthusiasm)

Boys, this is a spot of luck! Perhaps they can help us somehow!

(The MERMAID'S ISLE ROLLS ONSTAGE from STAGE LEFT, TRANSPORTING the three MERMAIDS, ETHEL, BUFFY, and GERTRUDE MERMAID. They sing happily away in three part harmony. ETHEL has a red beehive hairdo, heavy make-up, and long white gloves, and a glittering green mermaid suit complete with a long fan tail. She sits between her sisters and higher on the ISLE'S CORAL ROCKS. BUFFY is a blond, and GERTRUDE a brunette. Both have on the same basic outfits, with color differences and similar flashy accessories and make-up as ETHEL. There bodices should reveal some cleavage. ETHEL'S bodice could be fancier, and they should all sport flowers, starfish, and seashells in their hair and on their costumes. The ISLE itself is ROCKY CORAL with a spot of PALM TREES and GREENERY nestled on a SANDY, SHELL filled BEACH. As they sing, the MERMAID'S ISLE moves gracefully from STAGE LEFT to just RIGHT OF CENTER STAGE, directly in front of the ZEPPELIN to the three crew member's delight. SEYMOUR drops ANCHOR over the SIDE RAILING)

ETHEL, BUFFY, & GERTRUDE MERMAID

(Singing in three part harmony)

We are the Mermaid's of Mermaid's Isle / And have we got a rousing tale for you! / Just a few minutes ago, some pirates came along / And shot some crazy videos brand new / I'm Ethel, I'm Buffy, I'm Gertrude Mermaid / And boys you won't believe, those pirates were the scariest that we have ever seen / That poor girl that they kidnapped, a reporter we've been told / She screamed and screamed and screamed and screamed like the Sirens of legends old / And where do you suppose they're headed, those pirates and that poor girl? / To the Isle of Jaggar and Queen Thirteen, whose anger will surely unfurl / Queen Thirteen has imprisoned King Jaggar and the Fairies / And woe be to those who interfere, a wicked grudge that old Queen carries / She's a Fairy herself but was cast out of Fairyland long ago / For making a fuss by consorting with pirates and becoming the Fairies' foe / So, please, dear Doctor, don't go there, stay and chat with us a while / There's trouble there and we're lonely here, be a sport, come make us smile—isle, isle, isle, isle!

DOCTOR GEORGE

(Applauding, with joy and admiration)

Splendid, ladies, splendid, and thank you so much for the advice, but my crew and I must go to rescue Miss Junie Moon!

(The MERMAIDS show concern over the plight of JUNIE MOON)

ETHEL

Oh, yes, of course, that poor girl! Those horrible pirates confiscated her video camera. They stopped here briefly and intimidated us into performing embarrassing background melodies while forcing Miss Junie Moon to quote savage pirate statistics of their plundering and pillaging. All this, dear Doctor, while recording her shame on her own video camera!

SEYMOUR

Doctor George, what is Ethel Mermaid telling us? Is my darling in dire peril!

MAX

Haven't you been paying any attention, Seymour? It's in the 'Sirens Song.'

BUFFY

(Not too concerned, a little bored)

Oh yes, Jaggar's Isle—pirates love it there. Do you want us to reprise our 'Siren's Song' before you go?

GERTRUDE

(Nudging BUFFY)

Pipe down, Buffy, we're on a break! And, Ethel, clam up about those scurvy pirates--let's go for a swim—I need some fresh sea water to cleanse the stench those savage pirates left behind.

DOCTOR GEORGE

Oh, my stars! Are you saying that Captain Bandit the pirate has gone to Jaggar's Isle under the command of the tyrannical Queen Thirteen?

ETHEL

Yes, and they've captured all the Fairies in butterfly nets and put them in cages with King Jaggar himself! Queen Thirteen has totally taken over.

GERTRUDE

I'm afraid Queen Thirteen plans to feed them all, and your TV newscaster friend, to Jumper the Dragon!

BUFFY

Yeah, he's a big, green, scaly, fire breathing, scary dragon. He smokes, too.

SEYMOUR

Feed them all to Jumper the Dragon? Jeepers creepers—Junie Moon! My love! Oh…

(He faints, collapsing to the DECK, spasmodically thrashing his arms and legs)

DOCTOR GEORGE

This is diabolical! Max, prepare to ascend! Switch on the zeppelin mechanisms and gizmos for lift-off, and don't dilly-dally!

MAX

But, Doctor George, Sir, we can't stay aloft without the part I need.

(He holds up a small torn ROUND GASKET)

This gasket is shot, and I need a replacement. The hot air pressure will never hold without it!

BUFFY

Gee, Ethel, that gaskettie thing looks like one of your hooped earrings!

ETHEL

(Amazed, fiddling with one of her two earrings)

Why, so it does!

MAX

Dear ladies, what good fortune! Might I borrow that earring of yours for a while? It looks like a perfect match and is certain to do the trick and get us off the ground!

ETHEL

(Seductively)

Why certainly, Max, my sweet, I'm flattered.

(MAX takes the ring from her and begins his work)

DOCTOR GEORGE

Splendid! Thank you, Ethel Mermaid! And to both of you, too, Buffy and Gertrude—mercy be, you three darlings are ravishing, if you don't mind my saying so!

ETHEL

(She fluffs her red bouffant hairdo)

Thanks, sugar plum, your words titillate me. But Doctor, I only departed with my earing on one condition.

(She jingles her remaining earring with her fingers)

And I'll give you this one too, if you do as I ask.

DOCTOR GEORGE

Oh, what's that, pray tell, dear Ethel Mermaid?

ETHEL

(Alarmed, terrified)

You've got to take me and my sisters with you! We're helpless out here on Mermaid's Isle all by ourselves. There are sharks in the waters around here!

BUFFY

With big teeth!

GERTRUDE

And they have a lust for the taste of Mermaids. Our Mermaid's tails drive them wild!

ETHEL

Sharks prey on us constantly, but the tawdry advances of savage pirates like Captain Bandit and his plunder happy crew is nothing compared to the savagery of a hungry shark!

DOCTOR GEORGE

It's a relief to know you do not fear the pirates. Perhaps you can come along and help us by seducing them into returning Junie Moon to our care.

ETHEL

If those pirates came back we'd just hypnotize them with our 'Siren's Song.' They are the pussycats of the sea. We can wrap our tails around them!

(The MERMAIDS flip their MERMAID'S TAILS)

GERTRUDE

But think about this--we've got tails, Doctor George, tails!

BUFFY

And deadly sharks want them for dinner!

DOCTOR GEORGE

(Convinced and taking action)

Tails, by twitter—hop aboard, girls, times a wasting!

ETHEL

(Thankfully)

Hurry, and come along girls! All aboard! Don't forget your scales, flippers, and tails!

(THEY scurry ABOARD with a little help from MAX and DOCTOR GEORGE as SEYMOUR awakes from his faint)

SEYMOUR

(Delirious)

Land ho! Pirates ahead! Proceed with caution!

MAX

Seymour, give us a hand with the Mermaids! Hurry up and be a man!

SEYMOUR

Jeepers! What carnage those pirates threaten! I've never seen such blatant disrespect for hero's like us!

(Lusting after the MERMAIDS)

Oh—scales, incredible, luscious scales—oh, la la! What fantastic fantasy creatures have we here?

DOCTOR GEORGE

Pull yourself together, Seymour, and help Max get this zeppelin aloft.

ETHEL

(Seductively batting her eyes)

I'm glad you liked the part you ordered, Max. Hope it fit snuggly in place.

MAX

(Gulping nervously)

Thanks, ma'am, you're a lifesaver.

ETHEL

You're truly welcome. Just call me, Ethel, cutie.

MAX

(Blushing)

Aw shucks, Ethel, thanks a million.

(SEYMOUR and MAX go to work on the ZEPPELIN ENGINE)

ETHEL

Don't mention it, honey-bunch!

MAX

No, I wouldn't think of mentioning it. Help me out, Seymour, come on.

SEYMOUR

Ethel's okay, but my heart belongs to Junie Moon.

MAX

No, dummy, help me get this zeppelin aloft!

(ETHEL looks around with wonder at the ZEPPELIN)

ETHEL

Well, girls, what do you think about this bird?

BUFFY

Groovy, I mean, like wow! Look how big the balloon is!

GERTRUDE

Except it reminds me of the shape of a certain vegetable, hmm, could it be a large cucumber?

BUFFY

It looks more like a big sausage to me.

GERTRUDE

What do you think Doctor George had in mind when he designed this bird?

ETHEL

Well, Gertrude, it flies, and it looks like a boat, so maybe a duck or a goose?

BUFFY

Oh! You know, I always wanted to fly like those seagulls who taunt us on Mermaid's Isle when we sing our 'Siren's Song'.

DOCTOR GEORGE

Welcome aboard my Magnificent Zeppelin, beauteous Mermaids! I am at your service.

GERTRUDE

You're so kind, Doctor. When those sharks come around all we know to do is swim for our lives as fast as we can.

ETHEL

Thankfully, though, dolphins love us and do scare them away sometimes. Now those pirates are another story.

GERTRUDE

Oh, those pirates weren't so horrid, were they, Ethel? They shot videos of us from very unflattering angles, and made us flip our tails in a risqué manner, but other than kidnapping that TV reporter, what's the harm in that?

BUFFY

Yes, they're fresh, but then they're so cute, especially the one they call Laddie.

ETHEL

It was positively embarrassing, that's what, Buffy! I was purposely forced to sing off-key in order to scare them away!

GERTRUDE

Yes, Ethel, that was a big help—but don't you always sing off-key?

(ETHEL, insulted, GERTRUDE quickly recants)

I agree Ethel, those nasty pirates are scurvy chauvinists, but the one named Prince looked good to me.

BUFFY

Laddie's the handsome seaman of my deep sea dreams!

ETHEL

Girls, those pirates are the scourge of the sea! They are off limits! Of course, I was kinkily attracted to their leader, Captain Bandit—all those muscles, so rippled, bulging, and sinfully sensual.

(Embarrassed, pulling herself together)

Say, Doctor George, sweetie, how soon do we hit the skies?

DOCTOR GEORGE

No time at all, Ladies, the zeppelin will soon be aloft.

(MAX and SEYMOUR, still working on the RINGED VALVE and testing pressure by pulling LEVERS, release SMOKE and STEAM)

MAX

Eureka, she's fixed!

SEYMOUR

Nice going, Max! She's ready to fly, sir!

(The MERMAIDS all squeal with delight)

DOCTOR GEORGE

Fantastic! Good work, boys! Let's have lift-off! Man your stations! I'll take the wheel. Hold on tight to the railing, Ladies, we're off to rescue Junie Moon! With any luck, we'll have her and her documentary of our adventures back to the States in time for the eleven o'clock news!

(SEA, AIR, and LIGHTING EFFECTS begin as ACTION CONTINUES into ACT 1 – SCENE 4)

Act 1 – Scene 4

Off to Rescue Junie Moon

(The ZEPPELIN LIFTS OFF the SEA WAVES which move OFF RIGHT along with MERMAID'S ISLE. CLOUDS and BIRDS drift by serenely)

GERTRUDE

This is thrilling! We seaborne gals are now airborne gals!

BUFFY

Oh, I feel like a fish out of water! Thank you, Doctor George!

ETHEL

Don't you mean a flying fish, Buffy?

(EVERYONE reacts with adlibbed giggles and chatter after several FLYING FISH fly by, STAGE LEFT to RIGHT)

GERTRUDE

(Breaking the jovial mood)

Uh, Doc, there's just one problem.

DOCTOR GEORGE

Problem? Is there a problem, dear girl?

GERTRUDE

(Dryly, matter-of-fact)

We can only survive out of the water for short lengths of time, like when we're sunning ourselves on the coral rocks of Mermaid's Isle.

ETHEL

Don't let's be gloomy! That's a simple problem to fix, Doctor.

DOCTOR GEORGE

How so, my dear Ethel?

ETHEL

(Cheerfully)

It's easy! Just every so often fly us down near the water so we can take a little dip in the ocean!

DOCTOR GEORGE

But of course, why didn't I think of that? Come on everyone, we're on our way!

(Everyone cheers while the MERMAIDS reprise a THIRD VERSE of "DOCTOR GEORGE'S MAGNIFICENT ZEPPELIN" in three part harmony)

ETHEL, GERTRUDE, & BUFFY

He's Doctor George and oh! What a Magnificent Zeppelin / We're flying high, so high up into the skies / The six of us will surely have thrilling encounters / Let's flip our tails with glee at the clouds passing by / We will show those pirates a thing or two, Queen Thirteen beware / Splashy Stewardesses, that's what we are, and that is why we care / He's Doctor George, and oh! What a Magnificent Zeppelin / So come along…

DOCTOR GEORGE, MAX, & SEYMOUR

(Joining in, singing in three part harmony)

So come along!

ETHEL, GERTRUDE, & BUFFY

So come along / We're flying high…

DOCTOR GEORGE, MAX, & SEYMOUR

We're flying high…

ETHEL, GERTRUDE, & BUFFY

So very high / So high, so high…

DOCTOR GEORGE, MAX, & SEYMOUR

So high, so high…

ETHEL, GERTRUDE, & BUFFY

So very high…

DOCTOR GEORGE, MAX, & SEYMOUR

So very high…

EVERYONE

Up into the skies!

(SEYMOUR takes the CAPTAIN'S WHEEL and DOCTOR GEORGE scans the HORIZON through his TELESCOPE)

DOCTOR GEORGE

Land ho!

MAX

(Echoing him)

Land ho!

(MAX is dashing about securing ROPES. DOCTOR GEORGE *takes the* CAPTAIN'S WHEEL *from* SEYMOUR *who goes to help* MAX*)*

SEYMOUR

Land ho, ladies and gents, hang on tight!

ETHEL

Link tails, girls, this landing might scrape off some scales!

DOCTOR GEORGE

Prepare to drop anchor, Seymour!

(SEYMOUR obliges, tossing the ANCHOR OVERBOARD*)*

Release hot air pressure, Max! Set her down gently. Easy does it.

(MAX opens VALVES *and* STEAM *and* SMOKE *escape)*

BUFFY

Oh, this is scary—can you see any dragons, Doctor George? I hope there aren't any! Dragons can sauté my libido!

GERTRUDE

No dragons yet, Buffy, maybe they're out to lunch.

ETHEL

Fine, just as long as we're not their dessert dish!

(She shakes her hips. Amused, MAX *takes a deep breath and pulls himself together)*

MAX

Dear ladies, dishes you definitely are, but we have more important business, there may be great danger ahead. And Junie Moon is in dire peril!

(MAX winks at them, then runs to help DOCTOR GEORGE *and* SEYMOUR *land the* ZEPPELIN *on* JAGGAR'S ISLE*)*

BUFFY

Ethel, do you think we can help them rescue Junie Moon from that scary Captain Bandit?

GERTRUDE

Pirates are pushovers, of course we can, Buffy, you screwball. Have faith in the mission. Doctor George knows what he's doing.

ETHEL

Gertrude, let's all three be on our best behavior and follow Doctor George's commands. He's the man in charge, here, and I must say, hmm, what a man he is…I may have to do a little work on his super ego myself.

BUFFY

Okay, I'm scared of evil queens, and dragons, but not pirates; so I plan to focus on those sexy pirates, especially Laddie. Will this plan of ours fit into your plans, Doctor George?

DOCTOR GEORGE

Dear Ethel, Gertrude, and Buffy, there's nothing to fear. My invention will prevail. I have confidence in the power of dark matter, by thunder.

MAX

Seeing the power of dark matter at work in your invention should be quite interesting. I wish I had your confidence, Doc. This is all a bit sci-fi.

SEYMOUR

Oh, Doctor George, Max, we simply must rescue my precious Junie Moon! God knows what horrors she may be facing! She needs me to save her and make her mine, God help me.

DOCTOR GEORGE

Very astute, yes, Mr. Seymour…God knows. And may God help us all to achieve our goals, from within the smallest sub atomic particle of energy, to the farthest reaches of intergalactic space, may we dwell peacefully in your luminous garden.

(OMINOUS MUSIC SWELLS, LIGHTS DIM, and FADE TO BLACK)

* Intermission *

Act 2 – Scene 1

Thirteenland, & The Source of True Evil

(As the ENTRACTE MUSIC FADES, JAGGAR'S ISLE rolls on from STAGE LEFT in TWO SECTIONS, coming to a stop on BOTH SIDES of the ZEPPELIN. The PIRATES casually lay around on the ISLE'S ROCKY, CRAGGY SHORES cradled by a patch of BEACH SAND, STAGE RIGHT drinking WINE from JUGS while roasting MARSHMALLOWS over a small FIRE. The FOUR FAIRIES, WINKIE, DINKIE, TWINKIE, and KING JAGGAR are trapped in a large BIRD CAGE, STAGE LEFT. Behind the cage on the WAGON is a BACKGROUND suggestion of the foreboding FAIRIE CASTLE in the distance. The FAIRIES have wings, and, when speaking, a XYLOPHONE plays, and only the MERMAIDS, being fantasy creatures themselves, understand their xylophoneze language. Evil QUEEN THIRTEEN, not a true Fairie, can no longer speak xylophoneze as she lost her fantasy standing when she went bad, choosing evil as her raison d'être. CAPTAIN BANDIT jumps up, brandishing his SWORD when he spots the ZEPPELIN)

CAPTAIN BANDIT

(Threatening)

Hold it right there, you blustering blimp-ettes, I thought me boys and I blasted you out of the air with our cannon balls?

SEYMOUR

Gee, sir, they look kind of fierce!

MAX

Uh, sir, how about giving them a dose of this? This will fix their wagon!

(MAX hands DOCTOR GEORGE the HYPNOTIC UMBRELLA)

DOCTOR GEORGE

(Taking it)

Splendid idea, Max! Perhaps we can avoid a conflict and rescue Miss Moon peacefully.

CAPTAIN BANDIT

(Laughing at them)

Why, Doctor George, what a nice choice of weapons, but I prefer my sword!

(Brandishing his SWORD, laughing)

Prepare to attack, boys!

(LADDIE and PRINCE sit by passively, munching roasted MARSHMALLOWS over the FIRE)

Prince! Laddie! On your feet, mates! The picnic's over, you scurvy scum!

(At wits end, he stomps up and down)

Avast, ye maties!

(LADDIE and PRINCE get up slowly, stretch and yawn, and continue munching on the MARSHMALLOWS, licking their fingers)

PRINCE

But, Captain Bandit, Sir, aren't we entitled to a break once in a while. You think so, too, Laddie?

LADDIE

You is right, Prince! We's two is on a break Captain Bandit, you're captainship, Sir.

PRINCE

Besides, we're just relaxing a little before Queen Thirteen feeds Ms. Moon to Jumper the Dragon—that's a must see event we don't want to miss.

LADDIE

(Listlessly, sighing, and reflecting)

Too bad purdy Missy Junie Moonie's gonna be sacrificed, Captain. She'd a made a niceties' cabin girl on our piraties' ship! I'd so love orderin' her around and makin' her do me special favors.

(He giggles, nudging PRINCE)

PRINCE

Admit it Captain, her culinary skills have spoiled us. Her Spanish soufflé is ravishing and suits a savage pirate's dietary needs. My bowels thank her.

CAPTAIN BANDIT

(Aghast, totally flustered)

I said, "Avast, ye maties!" Not, "Half-assed, ye maties!" Attack them now, scum, or I'll carve you scurvy boobs up into tiny pieces and bake you into that Spanish soufflé!

PRINCE

(Offended)

Boobs are we, eh, Captain? You can't be meaning me! Laddie, perhaps, but definitely not I.

(Having been drinking that JUG of WINE, LADDIE is high as a kite, indulged in his own personal euphoria, and enjoying the hallucinatory MARSHMALLOWS)

LADDIE

(Savoring the last bite of MARSHMALLOW)

Okay, gimme me a minute. I'm getting ready—just a second more.

PRINCE

Touchy, isn't he, Laddie?

(Noticing the MERMAIDS)

Hey look, it's those cute Mermaid dames! Hi, girls! Talk about boobies, Captain!

ETHEL

(Hushed tone)

Don't pay any attention to them, girls. Our boobies are off limits to pirates! They were simply horrible to us earlier when they kidnapped Junie Moon. I'm not certain we can forgive them.

(To PRINCE, boldly)

Sorry, Mister Prince, you pirates can forget about obtaining any favors from us!

CAPTAIN BANDIT

That's quite all right, darlins, 'cause we're going to have to have our way with you, anyway. Attack, boys! Plunder, pillage, and ravish—in that order!

SEYMOUR

(Having another melt-down)

Come on, Doctor George, do something! We're all in grave danger! I've never been ravished before, but it sounds terrifying!

MAX

(Getting panicky himself)

Hurry, Doctor George, before they finish us all off!

DOCTOR GEORGE

Right you are, men!

(He opens the HYPNOTIC UMBRELLA and begins spinning it in the PIRATE'S direction)

CAPTAIN BANDIT

Expecting rain, Doc?

DOCTOR GEORGE

Look deep into my Hypnotic Umbrella, eh fellas? How about you, me, and the girls going for a stroll along the beach?

CAPTAIN BANDIT

Oh, how swell that is, but my mates and I have another plan for you? Attack, men!

(DOCTOR GEORGE speaks poetically, spinning the HYPNOTIC UMBRELLA in the PIRATE'S direction)

DOCTOR GEORGE

Silly Savages, stay where you are, and put away those daring daggers. Pleasant thoughts outsmart by far, while peace prevails on the Isle of Jaggar!

(To MAX and SEYMOUR)

How was that, boys? Did I make any sense? Is my hypnotic chant taking effect on subduing the pirates?

(Hypnotized, LADDIE and PRINCE sit down and start making SAND CASTLES)

CAPTAIN BANDIT

You scurvy scum, don't stare into that umbrella—it's a trick! Come, on, mates, get up! Show them what you're made of! Let's have some good clean bloody violence already!

(Flabbergasted, he walks away)

I give up! Nobody wants to be bad anymore.

(He sighs, exasperated, and turns to DOCTOR GEORGE)

Hope you're happy now, Doctor George! Look what you've done to my pirate crew! They've totally forgotten the pleasures of plundering, pillaging, and ravishing, for mercy's sake!

(To himself)

Whatever happened to savage terror on the high seas? I thought we were winning the war against happiness. What became of the agonizing horror of it all? Am I slipping?

(Playing in the SAND with PRINCE, ignoring CAPTAIN BANDIT, LADDIE gazes longingly in the MERMAIDS direction)

LADDIE

You fishy lookin' gals are so purrr-ty. Me 'n Prince can't taken our eyes often you. Please, won't you three fishy-gals come over here and play with us in the sand.

BUFFY

(Aghast, and repulsed)

Just because Doctor George made you nice doesn't mean we can be taken advantage of—so don't get any ideas, you perverse pirate primitives!

SEYMOUR

Good going, Sir! The pirates have been successfully pacified!

(He takes the HYPNOTIC UMBRELLA and puts it away)

Don't you girls pay any attention to those cowardly pirates. If Doctor George hadn't put a stop to their attack, me 'n Max would a whopped 'em good! Then they'd be good to you, 'cause Max and I made them do it—we're strong! We eat our Wheaties!

MAX

Speak for yourself, Seymour. I play tennis to stay in shape!

(MAX pulls out a very old WOODEN TENNIS RACKET with broken strings from seemingly NOWHERE, and bats YELLOW TENNIS BALLS STAGE LEFT, STAGE RIGHT, wildly towards the ONSTAGE CHARACTERS, and a few out into the AUDIENCE)

DOCTOR GEORGE

Seymour, what's going on with Max?

SEYMOUR

Beats me, Doc. He likes to play tennis.

BUFFY

Well where is his tennis court?

ETHEL

Watch it, Max, you'll ace us with that serve. Perhaps he's a little stressed.

GERTRUDE

Nice volley, Max, care to join us in a set of mixed doubles?

MAX

Sure, ladies, did you bring your rackets with you? That's why I'm strong! My killer serve and powerful forehand will blow those craggy old pirates away! You see, I had a personal plan of my own to initiate if Doctor George's divisive Hypnotic Umbrella gag—sorry--idea hadn't worked!

(EVERYONE ONSTAGE has been dodging TENNIS BALLS and looking at MAX like he's out of his mind. THEY have all been trying to catch, throw, and swat the TENNIS BALLS back to him. CAPTAIN BANDIT takes MAX'S RACKET and tosses it into the fire)

CAPTAIN BANDIT

Sorry, kid, that's set and match. Games over, run for cover!

GERTRUDE

You pirates are a lot of hot air! Just like the hot air in this Magnificent Zeppelin of Doctor George's!

(She looks down over the RAILING and swoons)

Oh, Buffy! I think I'm going to be land sick! I need salty sea air and water, fast!

ETHEL

Hang in there, girls, as soon as the good Doctor can save Junie Moon, I'm sure he'll give us the sea break we need. We're not used to all these hard rocky shores! Land-based individuals have no respect for ocean bound fantasy creatures!

SEYMOUR

Don't worry my Mermaid friends; I'm here to protect you! Seymour's here and he's not queer! Uh—

(Not sure of what he just proclaimed)

—So have no fear?

(SEYMOUR scratches his head, all the FAIRIES jingle with excitement in Xylophoneze from their BIRD CAGE, and DOCTOR GEORGE shakes his head wearily, contemplating SEYMOUR'S embarrassing proclamations)

DOCTOR GEORGE

Tsk, tsk, tsk, oh, my poor boy.

(Snapping to, forgetting they are in dire peril)

Oh, my stars, Max, set the Fairies free before Queen Thirteen shows up!

(Jumping up, LADDIE dashes to the BIRD CAGE to free them)

LADDIE

Me do, me do! I want to free the Fairies. I like Fairies! We pirates are the toughest and we'll do all the protecting. Hey, look at all the pretty Fairies! They're all better, now, 'cause I made friends with them!

(The FAIRIES kiss him and dance all over the STAGE, throwing GLITTER and speaking happily in Xylophoneze)

PRINCE

Watch it, Laddie, they're liable to convert you into a Fairie.

LADDIE

They like me! They really like me! Hi ya, Winkie, Dinkie, and Twinkie! Don't forget to obey your master, King Jaggar, King of the Fairies!

(KING JAGGAR FLIES into the air and jingles in Xylophoneze, anxiously pointing off STAGE LEFT)

MAX

Doctor George! King Jaggar has spotted something! He's trying to warn us!

(CAPTAIN BANDIT grabs LADDIE from flittering with the FAIRIES and throws him down on the SAND next to PRINCE)

CAPTAIN BANDIT

Now we've done it, Laddie! We're all in trouble! Can't you be more like your buddy Prince! At least he hasn't interfered with the Queen's Fairies. We're not supposed to free them, stupid, we were supposed to be guarding them! Queen Thirteen will feed us to Jumper the Dragon instead of them! All this because of that snotty news reporter, Junie Moon! Well, mates, I don't think so!

(He wrestles with LADDIE, who struggles to keep his place in the sand next to PRINCE, who now gets up and tries to help CAPTAIN BANDIT get him to his feet)

LADDIE

I was just minding my own business here playing in the sand! I didn't do anything! Come on, Captain Bandit, let's build a sand castle together. You can be the Daddy. I always wanted a Daddy—and a Mommy, too, come to think of it. Hey, maybe Junie Moon could be our Mommy! Gee, I miss my real Mommy, wherever she is.

(LADDIE sniffles and begins to cry and CAPTAIN BANDIT lets go of him in disgust. PRINCE settles back down to continue working on his SAND CASTLE)

PRINCE

Why don't we all just relax, Captain, and let our inner child take over.

CAPTAIN BANDIT

No, we are not therapists! My inner child walked the plank years ago. By the shark that bit me in the ass by surprise, we're pirates, we are! We don't need Mommies and Daddies!

(He begins to sulk, pacing back and forth)

Where did I go wrong? What have I done to deserve this? Am I losing my sense of wrong doing? Am I becoming a good pirate? Can there be such a thing as that—a noble pirate?

PRINCE

(Innocently)

Don't worry, Captain, even if we give up pirating, both Laddie and I will still love you!

(PRINCE and LADDIE continue to cavort happily in the SAND as the dancing FAIRIES join them, all frolicking happily. DOCTOR GEORGE checks OFF STAGE LEFT through his TELESCOPE)

DOCTOR GEORGE

By, George, I mean, by myself, he's right! Queen Thirteen's approaching!

(Grimly)

Everyone, prepare yourself for some un-pleasantries!

(JUMPER THE DRAGON drags on a SET PIECE from STAGE LEFT which is a PLATFORM supporting JAGGED ROCK POSTS with JUNIE MOON LASHED between them like Fay Wray in the original "King Kong." JUMPER is a big, green, scaly dragon, wearing a SUNDIAL for a WRISTWATCH which has a BIG THIRTEEN at the top of the DIAL instead of the usual number twelve. With a ROPE over his shoulder, he pulls the SACRIFICIAL ALTAR ONSTAGE carrying JUNIE MOON CENTER STAGE where he pauses to rest. JUNIE MOON has been screaming incessantly and JUMPER, exhausted, incredulous of her shrieking display of fear, and unwilling to take it anymore, puts his claws on his hips, and addresses her directly. He steps back, feigning surprise, focusing on JUNIE MOON for several moments)

JUMPER

I've had just about enough of you, young lady, so you might as well save your screams for when dinner is served—and you are the main course!

(He puts his claws over his ears to suppress her incessant shrieking)

Goodness, are you any relation to Ethel Mermaid? I've never heard such a volume of noise, but I still think Fay Wray has you beat! Her shrieks were easily a few decibels higher than yours in the original King Kong, so I think the auditions are over for the next remake, Miss Moon!

ETHEL

I resent that remark, Mr. Jumper the Dragon! My vocal tones are never shrieks, and their decibels are always tolerably pleasant!

(In the style of ETHEL MERMAN from her 20th Century musicals 'Happy Hunting' and 'Gypsy' she belts out a coupled verse while BUFFY and GERTRUDE wince, plugging their ears)

Gee, but it's good to be here! And everything's coming up roses, this time for me—for me! For me! For meeeeeee!

BUFFY

Oh, Ethel, my goodness, are you summoning the whales?

GERTRUDE

Save it for the concert back on Mermaid's Isle, Miss McDiva.

JUMPER

Sorry, Miss Ethel Mermaid, I hadn't really noticed you standing there with your school-girl chorus of fish-ettes. You do sing a tantalizing Siren's Song.

(He licks his chops, salivating, ogling the Mermaids)

I always was partial to seafood.

(Addressing JUNIE MOON)

I may have to save you for dessert instead of the main course!

(Running to flirt with the MERMAIDS)

Because the main course just arrived on this blimp here!

(Taking in the ZEPPELIN, he moves to admire the entire scene)

My, you ladies of the deep blue sea certainly like to travel in style! Forget the Chickens of the Sea—Meet the Chickie-Pies of the Skies! Do you Chickie-Pies mind if I make you the first course instead of Miss Junie Moon here?

ETHEL

We certainly do! And, if you know what's good for you, you green scaly monstrosity, you'll keep your big mouth shut and go on a diet! You're a little too green around the gills for our taste in fire breathing dragons!

JUMPER

(Claws to his cheeks in mock horror)

I didn't think it showed! Humph! You three have twice the scales as I do.

(Holding his SUNDIAL WRISTWATCH to the SUN)

Tempus fugit, Miss Junie Moon, and you, too, Chickie-Pies of the Skies, for when the sundial shadows thirteen, it'll be dinner time, which will be any minute now, so if I were you, Screaming-Lady, or you three Chickie-Pies-of-the-Skies, I'd begin by saying grace!

(He puts his claws together in prayer)

Dear Heavenly Dragonfly, for this scrumptious female I am about to decease, may the devouring begin on this delectable feast. Hi did ally ho, my woo-man and I, the beatific beast!

(He does a little swirl with his claws)

JUNIE MOON

(Pleading for help)

Oh, Doctor George, you're just in time to save me before Jumper the Dragon begins the disgusting task of rendering my innocent virginal flesh to bare bones! Thirteen o'clock is only but moments away!

(SEYMOUR tosses out the GANGPLANK)

SEYMOUR

(Great show of courage)

I'm coming for you, Junie Moon! Never fear, Seymour's not queer, and he's finally here!

(SEYMOUR trips down at the bottom of the GANGPLANK doing a forward roll into the BEACH SAND, landing spread eagle. EVERYONE ONSTAGE rolls their eyes, shaking their heads at Seymour's naiveté)

MAX

(Amused)

Didn't wet your pants, did you, Seymour?

JUMPER

(Checking his SUNDIAL WATCH)

Look, everyone, its thirteen o'clock! Could somebody please ring the dinner bell?

(Going over to JUNIE MOON, licking his chops)

Oh, yummy, such a tasty morsel you are, my dear Miss Moon—nothing I like better than saucy TV journalist over-easy! A bit famishing-femme-fatal, don't you think?

(JUMPER nudges SEYMOUR with his foot)

SEYMOUR

(Jumping to his feet)

Stand back, you green scaly barbeque pit torch!

(Running to JUNIE MOON, he loosens her BONDS and she flees)

Run for your life, my darling lover to be!

JUMPER

Hey, cut that out! Talk about a quick bite—it's not polite to steal the eats and run you know, and I didn't even get a chance to lick the spoon!

(JUNIE MOON dashes ON BOARD the ZEPPELIN)

DOCTOR GEORGE

Are you okay, Miss Moon?

JUNIE MOON

(Breathlessly)

Yes, thank you, Doctor George, but I'm afraid I lost my video camera to the pirates and won't be able to make my award winning documentary about your adventures.

DOCTOR GEORGE

That's quite all right, I doubt if anyone would believe them.

(The MERMAIDS and MAX continue to cheer on SEYMOUR. He has been trying to get JUMPER tied up in JUNIE MOON'S place between the STONE POSTS ALTAR. They cavort about in a tug of war with a bit of ROPE, reminiscent of musical chairs, alternately lashing each other between the POSTS, but neither succeeding)

MAX

Come on, Seymour, you can do it! Sack that slimy scaly green lizard!

JUMPER

(Taking offense)

Slimy? Watch your language! That hurts, you know!

BUFFY

Seymour, you're the most! I have scales, too, and they need you to stroke them.

GERTRUDE

(Also admiring him, though jealously)

My, what a handsome heroic specimen of manhood you are, Mr. Green Dragon Slayer. When Buffy's through with you, I'll be in the wings, flipping my tail suggestively.

BUFFY

Or telling tales! Lay off the hero types, Gertrude, or they might suggest you take a cold swim into shark infested waters.

JUMPER

(Accepting their compliments by mistake)

You delightful Chickie-Pies flatter me. I try to work out three times a week which keeps me from getting too slimy or scaly. I do crunches in the morning to tighten the belly—the bones from last night's meal are a good source of fiber.

(Grabbing SEYMOUR)

Will you please hold still long enough for me to torch you with my secret weapon!

(He huffs and puffs, sputters and spits, but no smoke and flames emerge from his jaws.)

Guess my pilot light must have gone out! Have you got a match, Seymour?

(Shaking his head 'no,' Jumper searches his own pockets)

SEYMOUR

Gee, I'm sorry, Jumper, I quit smoking after I graduated from high school.

MAX

Yeah, I remember the vice-principal catching you in the men's room. Your wimpy coughing spells gave you away.

SEYMOUR

Girls liked a guy who smoked, I got more dates than you ever did!

MAX

I don't think so, Seymour—as if—no girls went near you as I recall. Nerds who smoke are still just nerds.

JUMPER

That's okay, Seymour, I understand, I was never popular at Green Dragon High School on the east side of Jaggar's Isle. Oh, the memories! Takes me back a long, long way. You and Max have your whole lives ahead of you. Don't let the years pass you by lest you end up chewing on old bones like yours truly.

(Checking yet another one of his pockets)

This is my lucky day! I have a matchbook in my backside pouch.

(He takes out a matchbook, strikes a match, and SMOKE and FLAMES shoot out from his mouth)

I wish I could stop smoking like you did, Seymour. But it's part of my nature. Once a dragon, always a dragon. C'est la vie!

ETHEL

Hey, someone stop him, he'll barbeque Seymour! Why don't you lazy pirates do something to stop this carnage? Give Seymour a hand!

CAPTAIN BANDIT

(Applauding, sarcastically)

Nice work, Seymour! You'd make a great pirate if you weren't so shrimpy! Anyone for shrimp scampi à la Seymour? Go, Jumper, go, and scorch that scurvy cabin boy!

ETHEL

You call that helping him? Seymour's no shrimp, he's all man!

MAX

Sorry, Seymour, once a shrimp, always a shrimp.

CAPTAIN BANDIT

I gave him a hand, didn't I?

(Glaring at his PIRATE CREW playing in the SAND)

Hey guys, let's go dig for buried treasure! You remember, don't you? Buried Treasure? Remember, that's one of our primary goals in life!

LADDIE

Oh, boy, bring me a shovel, Daddy! Gee, my fingernails are getting kinda dirty.

CAPTAIN BANDIT

Tsk, tsk, tsk, what will Mommy say? Excuse me, I've got to go and see if Mommy knows where I left my shovel. Oh, Queenie! Mrs. Thirteen! You're Majesty-Ship!

(CAPTAIN BANDIT exits STAGE LEFT to find QUEEN THIRTEEN)

PRINCE

Hey, Seymour, if you need any help, just ask. Hey, Laddie, you like to wrestle dragons?

LADDIE

Sure, just as soon as I'm finished building my castle.

ETHEL

I think you pirates have your heads in the sand.

BUFFY

You tell 'em, Ethel Mermaid! They're too drunk to fight Jumper the Dragon.

GERTRUDE

Well, I'm just not going to stand here and watch Seymour get scorched!

ETHEL

Let's help somehow, girls, there must be something we can do.

(GERTRUDE pulls a FISH out of her BODICE, reaches out over the RAILING, and bops JUMPER on the snout)

GERTRUDE

Take that, you lout! Smoked trout is much better for the digestion, Jumper. And I never cared for shrimp, so leave Seymour alone!

JUMPER

(Reeling from the whack on the snout)

Foul, foul! Or should I say, trout, trout! Ouch, that smarts! No fair fishing from the sidelines, girls! Oh, and it smells pungent, too, like smoked fish—but that's another entre I hadn't considered. Jeepers, I think she put out my fire. Fudge cakes!

(To GERTRUDE, whining soulfully)

Come on, lady, lighten up on my fire! Oh, Gertrude! Come on baby, light my fire!

(JUMPER starts to dance since the last line reminds him of the song "Light My Fire." As he dances, he gives SEYMOUR a chance to finally succeed in tying him up between the POSTS. All the while, EVERYONE has begun dancing to the tune. The FAIRIES dance with joy, jingling happily around JUMPER. KING JAGGAR FLIES about the STAGE, jingling merrily in Xylophoneze. This gives Seymour a chance to succeeding in restraining JUMPER)

SEYMOUR

Ha, ha! How does it feel to be lashed to the spit like a barbecued chicken?

JUMPER

Finger licking good?

(Getting worried)

Now, come on, Seymour, Doctor George, Max, this really isn't fair! I was only going to take a teensy weensy bite outta her! She wouldn't have felt a thing! Junie Moon would've been fine!

(More anxious)

This is no way to treat a dragon! It's humiliating for starters. What's Queen Thirteen going to say when she gets here? She'll strip off my lovely green scales one by one—and I'll be naked!

(KING JAGGAR FLIES to the ZEPPELIN jingling fiercely in Xylophoneze. The rest of the FAIRIES join him on the ZEPPELIN)

DOCTOR GEORGE

Unfortunately, I don't speak Xylophoneze, so I'm not certain what the fuss is all about.

ETHEL

Only fantasy creatures can understand Xylophoneze, Doctor George.

BUFFY

And we qualify!

GERTRUDE

Yes, we Mermaids of Mermaid's Isle can speak it fluently!

ETHEL

King Jaggar says we better take off before his wife, her majesty Queen Thirteen, gets here. Since she turned bad, she can only speak like mortals, and what she has to say I don't think any of us want to stick around to hear!

GERTRUDE

She has terrible magic powers aimed to terrorize and destroy!

BUFFY

So what are we hanging around here for? My tail's a flippin'!

JUMPER

Flippin', floppin', let's get hoppin' and split! Set me free somebody or Queenie will scale me alive!

SEYMOUR

No way, Jumper, you can't be trusted after trying to flame-broil Junie Moon!

JUMPER

Simmer down, you hot headed show off! Set me free and let me come with you. You'll never have to eat fried food again, because I flame broil everything. We'll be so trim and slim no one will recognize us.

SEYMOUR

I'm not sure I can trust a dragon.

MAX

Maybe it would be a good idea, Seymour. Doctor George, it might be a good idea to have a dragon on our side.

DOCTOR GEORGE

Good thinking, Max.

JUMPER

You'll never have to eat out—think of the money you'll save! I cook, I clean, I do dishes—I even wash windows!

(JUNIE MOON rushes down the GANGPLANK to untie JUMPER)

JUNIE MOON

What a bonus, good help is hard to find these days! With my busy schedule as an attractive TV newscaster, I never have time for my domestic duties.

(Enthusiastically to JUMPER)

I have a guest room you'll just love with a great view of the ocean.

(Condescendingly)

I'm up at five a.m., and I take my breakfast at six a.m. I'm on the air at seven with the morning news, so I like my coffee strong!

(JUNIE MOON escorts JUMPER up the GANGPLANK as MAX observes JUNIE MOON'S new haughty takeover persona)

MAX

You've been outclassed, Seymour, unless of course you are also up at the crack of dawn and like to do windows.

DOCTOR GEORGE

Welcome aboard, Jumper, my scaly green friend! Fire up the zeppelin, Max! To your stations, Seymour! I suggest we take King Jaggar and Winkie, Dinkie, and Twinkie's advice and escape while we can!

JUMPER

Oh, thank you so much you, Doctor George. I was getting tired of chomping the heck out of Queen Thirteen's victims. That's a guilt trip complex you wouldn't believe, and I personally don't wish it on anyone—even Queen Thirteen herself. You know, she had me toiling for thirteen hours a day! Thirteen! Imagine that! How was I supposed to get any rest?

ETHEL

(Sympathetically)

You must have been exhausted, Jumper, or should I say extinguished?

SEYMOUR

(Not getting it)

Thirteen hours a day? Is that possible?

JUMPER

Around here it is—and without a break!

(JUMPER checks his SUNDIAL WATCH)

You see, in Thirteenland, formally known as Jaggar's Isle, there's thirteen hours a day. Oh, my, it's just thirteen o'clock now, see?

(He shows his SUNDIAL WATCH to everyone nearby)

And, If you all hadn't come along in the nick of time—

JUNIE MOON

(Startled)

—I'd be dinner!

(EVERYONE gasps with horror at the revelation of JUNIE MOON being dinner. Suddenly, a FLASH BOMB explodes OFF STAGE LEFT and QUEEN THIRTEEN ENTERS through the SMOKE followed by CAPTAIN BANDIT, who is VIDEOGRAPHING her and the following action with JUNIE MOON'S VIDEO CAMERA. QUEEN THIRTEEN is dressed gaudily in a spiky outfit of black, purple, orange, yellow, and red, and she carries a MAGIC SCEPTER with an ORNATE GLOBE DEVICE on the end of it which can PULSATE and FLASH whenever she activates it. EVERYONE reacts with continued horror as LADDIE and PRINCE leap to their feet and dash ON BOARD the ZEPPELIN. GERTRUDE and BUFFY leap into their arms in the hopes that they will all then be rescued)

CAPTAIN BANDIT

(Furious at his crew)

So, it's mutiny, eh, boys? Shiver me timbers, you know what that means, don't you?

PRINCE

Well, either we're very cold, or you want us to walk the plank.

LADDIE

No, not the plank! We'll fall off the end of the world and into the sea and drown! Save us, Doctor George! Take us with you! We promise to be good! We'll never pillage, plunder, or ravish ever, ever again!

(He spits in his hand and raises it)

Pirate's honor!

ETHEL

Strike while the iron's hot, girls, when they're the most vulnerable—you can work on changing them later to satisfy you after you're both married!

GERTRUDE

(Lovingly to PRINCE, who holds her tight)

Save me, you scourge of the sea. Meow, I just love a big burly man with tacky tattoos all over his hunky muscled body!

BUFFY

(Seductively to LADDIE)

The eye patches and colorful pirate bandanas are a plus!

(JUNIE MOON clutches tightly to SEYMOUR while MAX hides behind the CAPTAIN'S STEERING WHEEL, where DOCTOR GEORGE stands firm, resilient and fearless)

MAX

(Apprehensive, a hint of sarcastic)

Doctor George, got any more brilliant ideas? That Hypnotic Umbrella gag worked well earlier.

DOCTOR GEORGE

Try not to panic, everyone. Remain calm. Our mission was, naturally, not to run in fear, but to face our enemies head on. Hmm, I seem to have lost my train of thought in the midst of all the excitement.

(He falters, grimaces, strikes a pose of defiance, then falters)

I'll think of something rest assured. I hope, hmm, it has something to do with the mission. So as soon as I collect my thoughts on the matter, I'll....

(As DOCTOR GEORGE shuffles around uselessly, CAPTAIN BANDIT continues to videograph the scene)

QUEEN THIRTEEN

Try and shoot me from my left side only, it makes me look meaner.

(To EVERYONE on the ZEPPELIN)

Who among you let my husband and those Fairies out of their bird cage? And why hasn't that prissy newscaster been reduced to bare bones by my dragon, Jumper? Speak up, anyone!

JUMPER

(Helplessly, clueless)

I'm on a diet?

QUEEN THIRTEEN

Silence! Or I'll zap you with my pure evil high voltage magic scepter!

(She waves her SCEPTER in his direction, and each time she thrusts it forward, JUMPER cringes)

BUFFY

Golly, she's ugly! What kind of getup is that she has on, talk about tacky!

(KING JAGGAR jingles fearfully and FLIES over to hide behind the defiant DOCTOR GEORGE)

GERTRUDE

(Shushing BUFFY)

Buffy, be still! Where are your manners? King Jaggar says his wife is merely misguided. She won't hurt us, Prince, now will she?

LADDIE

(To BUFFY in his arms)

If we're gonna die, can we get married first, Buffy, sweetie?

PRINCE

I don't know, Laddie, the single life leaves more time for looting and pillaging—not to mention, ravishing—you'd miss that, wouldn't you!

(To GERTRUDE, who eyes him with intimidation)

Gertrude, you salty sea-wench, would you consider forgoing marriage instead so that we can continue on with our chosen lifestyle?

(Still fearful, intimidated by the overall situation, she capitulates)

GERTRUDE

Sure, sure, anything you want, already! But forget about the ravishing, Prince, that's definitely out. Mermaids forbid that kind of stuff. But pillage if you must—go crazy—just get Buffy and I the heck outta here!

(QUEEN THIRTEEN is waving her MAGIC SCEPTER around)

QUEEN THIRTEEN

(Menacingly)

Silence, trespassers! Anyone who tries to escape gets zapped! You are my prisoners for life, doomed to slave away in my Hot House Trinket Factory!

JUNIE MOON

Oh, fruit squishies, with Captain Bandit having stolen my video camera, how will I ever be able to finish documenting this adventure?

QUEEN THIRTEEN

Silence, you vacuous video vixen!

ETHEL

Pardon me, Miss Thirteen, err, you're Eloquence. Just exactly what is expected of us in this so called Trinket Hot House of yours?

QUEEN THIRTEEN

(Brandishing her SCEPTER at ETHEL)

Silence! That's Queen Thirteen to you, Miss Diva from Mermaid's Isle! Defy me, you siren singing fillet of femme fatal, and I'll fillet your soul!

(To EVERYONE)

You will all discover my Hot House momentarily! Jumper the Dragon will escort all of you zeppelin zanies to my dungeon on Queen Thirteenland!

(To JUMPER, who goes to her reluctantly)

And remind me later, my gastro-inflammable goon, to have your green scales scraped against the grain for disobedience!

JUMPER

(Ever fearful, trembling)

Yes, yes, you're Thirteen-ship, ma'am, uh, Queenie! But if you'd care to reconsider my punishment, I promise to be good, er, bad! Bad! And I'll never let it happen again.

(To himself, bent on believing)

I'm bad, bad, bad to the bone!

QUEEN THIRTEEN

Silence, you scaly green traitor, only negative thinking is allowed here on the Isle of Jaggar—soon to be renamed 'Queen Thirteenland'—where promises are always made to be broken!

(She paces about, taking command of the stage, laying out her dire plans with relish)

I have generously created a genuine tourist trap on these very rocky shores! Visitors, who come here lured by the sordid, irresistible commercials of prancing and dancing Fairies, won't be allowed to leave until they've spent their life savings on worthless trinkets in my many souvenir gift shops. If they refuse to cough up the cash for trinkets, they'll end up like you trespassers, sweating it out thirteen hours a day for life in my Hot House Trinket Factory—a dank, dark, dungeon-like atmosphere for churning out endless millions of additional tasteless trinkets and souvenirs for my irresistible, enticing gift shops!

(She becomes a teacher in a classroom)

If there's one thing I've learned about traveling parents with screaming, multi-brat infested families bent on traveling to exotic vacation paradises, it's that they cannot leave without spending their money on worthless souvenirs and junk trinket-designed memorabilia. The vacationers who end up as prisoners in my Hot House Trinket Manufacturing Project will not be paid a salary. In lieu of wages, they will only be supplied with a small daily ration of stale bread and water.

(She looks around for support, then shrugs)

I'm sorry, but that's all I could afford. I'm on a tight budget, understand? How else can I raise millions for myself alone? Call it capitalism, free enterprise, or better yet, trinket-down-economics. Maybe you might think I'm leaning a little too far to the right, but Republican I'm not. But right, or not so right, I'm the only one who's going to have any rights around here! This is not a democracy after all, not like that U.S. of A you mongrels come from.

MAX

Not Republican? So what's with the trinket down economics? Doctor George, have you been listening to all this?

(She grumbles, turns to address the theatre audience directly, while MAX surreptitiously sneaks over to retrieve the HYPNOTIC UMBRELLA)

QUEEN THIRTEEN

Sorry if these acts of cruelty surrounding my enterprise remind you of terrorism. That's just the way the cookies crumble around here, so get used to it!

MAX

Psst, Doctor George, Sir, wouldn't this be an opportune time for the old, you know, Hypnotic Umbrella trick?

DOCTOR GEORGE

What was that, Max? What trick is that?

JUNIE MOON

Your invention that helped Seymour be brave!

DOCTOR GEORGE

But of course—my invention—yes, by Thunder, yes! My greatest invention of all!

MAX

Here you are, Doc, the perfect device for eliminating tyrants.

(MAX hands him the HYPNOTIC UMBRELLA, but he refuses it)

DOCTOR GEORGE

(Recovering confidence)

Thank you, Max, your heart is in the right place, but I think we need something a bit more persuasive! Bring me that crate next to the pickle barrel. Seymour, would you be so kind as to assist your crewmate, Max?

SEYMOUR

Yes, Sir!

(SEYMOUR and MAX carry the CRATE down the GANGPLANK to CENTER STAGE followed by DOCTOR GEORGE. QUEEN THIRTEEN eyes the activity suspiciously)

DOCTOR GEORGE

Seymour, Max, what are you waiting for? Give Her Majesty the lovely gift we've brought, especially designed for a thriving terrorist tourist-tyrant's egotistical needs!

(QUEEN THIRTEEN, suspicious, ZAPS a FLASH BOMB at their feet)

QUEEN THIRTEEN

Hold it right there! Not so fast! What's the name of this present you've brought for me, Doctor George?

DOCTOR GEORGE

(Proudly becomes a carnival barker)

Why, this is my incredible Vanity-Ego-Reflector, the perfect gift for terrorists and tyrants on the go! This indispensable-boudoir-accessory is the perfect compliment for evil dictators everywhere! It's a tantalizing gift specifically designed with sociopaths like you in mind, you're Majesty!

(He leans towards her confidentially)

It's a little something to ease the tension after a long day of evil misdeeds?

QUEEN THIRTEEN

(Indulging him with skeptic eyes)

Interesting, Doctor George, interesting, and it's not even my birthday! Let me see what you have here to entertain me. I won't believe it, dear Doctor George, until I see it with my own eyes, ha, ha!

DOCTOR GEORGE

Now open the crate, fellows, and carefully remove the Vanity-Ego-Reflector for Queen Thirteen's approval!

QUEEN THIRTEEN

Approval? Ha! I warn you, Doctor, I'm never in a mood for jokes. When I laugh, I only laugh manically at the contemplation of the fate of my doomed victims—make no mistake about that!

(SEYMOUR and MAX remove the GLITTERING, LIGHTED, FRAMED, MIRRORED DEVICE which can take on a life of its own like a children's electronic toy with dazzlingly LIGHT EFFECTS. This DEVICE can react to the characters dialogue. It can EMIT ODD SOUNDS like POPS and SQUEAKS. It is a thrilling sight for EVERYONE ONSTAGE, ALL gasping in amazement, except the unimpressed QUEEN THIRTEEN, who simply chortles with bemusement)

GERTRUDE

(Approving, awestruck)

Oh, Buffy, look! A magic mirror! Mirror, mirror, on the wall....

(She jiggles her behind, touches it, then sucks her finger)

Hmm, the perfect accessory for any seductive Mermaid.

BUFFY

(Gasping, filled with misgivings)

It looks dangerous! I'm homesick for Mermaid's Isle, Gertrude, let's split!

ETHEL

Although it might be great for our dressing room when we do our act at sea, I'm beginning to agree with Buffy.

(Panicking, she attempts to rally the Mermaids)

Girls! We've got tails for a reason, let's dive into the ocean and swim for home! We can skip this diabolical final act!

(KING JAGGAR scorns his wife, QUEEN THIRTEEN, jingling angrily in XYLOPHONEZE. She swats at him as if he were an annoying bug)

QUEEN THIRTEEN

What's that butterfly of a husband saying to me? Be gone! Get away! You are such a nuisance! When will the divorce be finalized for pity's sake!

ETHEL

King Jaggar says you should give the mirror to us, because it's not 'big enough' to reflect someone whose 'ego' is already the size of the Moon!

QUEEN THIRTEEN

I must be improving. Thank you, dear hubby. Is there anything else on your glittery little insect of a mind? Yes? No? I thought not.

ETHEL

He says no one will come to Thirteenland because he and all the Fairies would rather die than slave away in your Factory, Dungeon, Hot House, Trinket, and Souvenir Manufacturing Plant.

(She pauses for a breath)

That was a mouthful.... The Fairies have no desire to make callous, commercial baubles to attract innocent tourists to Thirteenland!

(QUEEN THIRTEEN aims her SCEPTER at KING JAGGAR. It PULSATES and FLASHES, SPARKING a BRIGHT SMOKE BOMB that goes off between them, horrifying EVERYONE)

JUMPER

Eek, that was a close one, girl!

(Hands on hips, dryly)

Ya know, Queenie, dear, I'm a fantasy creature, too, and I think what your hubby meant to say was, er....

(About to be zapped, he retreats back up the GANGPLANK)

My, don't you look really fabulous in that getup! Early Spanish Inquisition, is it?

QUEEN THIRTEEN

Traitorous reptile, take that!

(The RAILING next to him gets ZAPPED. He screams, runs behind JUNIE MOON, and holds onto her)

JUMPER

Gee whiz, you're Majesty, can't you take a compliment? Save me Miss Moon, take me to your apartment now! I'll start with the kitchen floor. I bet it's just as untidy as can be and needs scrubbing, mopping and a thick coat of wax! Did I mention I do dishes?

DOCTOR GEORGE

My dear Majesty, Queen Thirteen, I'm sure your subject, Jumper the Dragon, meant no hard feelings in complimenting you just now. As far as my crew, Miss Moon, and certainly I are concerned; your Hot House Trinket Factory would not bother us in the least! We are a hearty bunch from the United States of America, a land free of terrorist attacks only because of our constant vigilance against them, and of your ilk, which spawns them. We are quite used to the stress and strain, fear and trauma, which representatives of evil such as you present to the world. To tolerate, and yet suppress you, is our primary goal and duty—and we will not shirk it!

(SEYMOUR, MAX, and JUNIE MOON are noticeably bewildered)

SEYMOUR

Are you talking about us, Doctor George?

(To himself, helplessly)

Jeepers, creepers, where's the U.S. Military when you need them?

MAX

Is this our responsibility as citizens of the glorious U.S.A., Doctor George, Sir, and have you thought this through? You are referring to little old us, I assume. Is it then our responsibility alone to stop all evil just because we're from the United States of America?

JUNIE MOON

Max has got a point, honestly, Doctor, have you lost your mind? Surely you can't think to include me. I'm quite satisfied with my position as a sexy newscaster scavenging sensational stories for W.H.O.P. TV. I can't be expected to vanquish terrorists! I just report and videograph their sadistic antics! It's my duty as a reporter, to exaggerate and exploit the horrific shenanigans of such evildoers, not to personally subdue them myself. My responsibility, Doctor, is to whip up fearful, hysterically slanted public opinion against terrorists, so that our Federal Government can then point the way to solutions to engage military action! If not, then what's the point of having an economically inflated military industrial complex! A lot of U.S.A. taxpayer money is spent to secure our country and the entire world with the mightiest and toughest military! We can't be expected to fight them as brave citizens ourselves! That's why we have a Pentagon!

QUEEN THIRTEEN

(Laughing maniacally)

Of course not, ha, ha, ha! Television journalism will only serve to help me execute my plans! Doctor George, you amaze me! Mortals such as you are such fools. Americans are all couch potatoes glued to their televisions. Thirteenland TV commercials will point up all the fun of terror, horror, and violence in our society. The public will not be able to resist the lure of barbarianism; humans have a natural lust for the sport of aggressive savagery. That's why I'm certain they will flock like sheep to Thirteenland, excited, thrilled, and eager to meet their inevitable doom! Ha, ha, ha!

(She brandishes her SCEPTER majestically to all her captives)

But before I send all of you to my Hostile Hot House Sweat Shop, let me partake of this little gift you've brought to me all the way from the United States of America—that pitiful capitalist burg of accidental tourists.

BUFFY

(Hysterical)

And we tourists don't want to be her next accident! Give her the gift, Doctor, so we can fly up into the skies, and ride this kooky flying fish out of here!

GERTRUDE

I'm no tourist, but it's no accident I've have been around the island a few times. Give Her Majesty her gift and, if she likes it, maybe she'll leave us alone!

PRINCE

I don't think we can count on that happening. She hates everything.

MAX

Shouldn't we all be running for our lives?

SEYMOUR

Look into it, Queen Thirteen, please! Don't you evil Queens generally like fancy mirrors?

ETHEL

Take the gift already you're Majesty, and let us all go!

BUFFY

Do you think she'll hate the present you've brought her?

LADDIE

Oh, yeah, Buffy, Prince said so, she hates everything!

(QUEEN THIRTEEN has had enough. With a thrust of her SCEPTER a FLASH BOMB explodes CENTER STAGE)

QUEEN THIRTEEN

Silence! If this is indeed a gift and not some fancy failsafe device, then let Miss Junie Moon test it out for me first!

(JUMPER screams, runs behind JUNIE MOON, holding onto her)

JUNIE MOON

Jimmie Crickets, Doctor George, dare I glance into the Vanity-Ego-Reflector? I don't want to end up like TV gossip queen, Gloria Glamorude, and lose my savvy news-junky edge!

JUMPER

Don't do it, Junie Moon! It might damage your glamour factor! Who is this Gloria Glamorude anyway? Is she related to Barbara Walters?

(Lisping)

Hi, everyone, my name is Gloria Glamorude, the rudest woman in all of Fairieland. Look for my ribald raunchy reporting in my next repugnant primetime presentation! Rude, baby, rude!

DOCTOR GEORGE

(Comforting)

There's nothing to fear, Miss Moon, as long as you don't mind seeing yourself as you really are. I got quite a kick out of it myself when I first gazed into its mystical, glassy, reflective depths.

JUNIE MOON

(Shrugging, then smiling bravely)

Oh, well, in that case, what have I got to lose?

(She goes towards the VANITY-EGO-REFLECTOR and JUMPER leaps in front of her)

JUMPER

Don't do it, I tell you! Your fragile ego might crack!

(Blocking her, he begins staring into its REFLECTIVE DEPTHS where LIGHTS SPIN, SPIRAL, and FLASH colorfully as gusting AIR, CONFETTI, and GLITTER rush past him)

What a lovely green suit of scales you have with such a noble snout for spewing smoke and flames. And just look at this tail of mine! Have you ever in your life seen such a magnificent tail as this? Oh-oh my, yes, yes, yes, I suppose I did chomp a few too many innocent Fairies, but I was just following orders. But then, that's no excuse is it? Yes, yes, I must take personal responsibility for my actions of the past. Please, forgive me, I didn't mean to do it! Those naughty Fairies never tasted that great anyway! I'm begging you to forgive me! I can change, believe me, I can change! I'll never, never harm any innocent Fairie creatures ever again! I promise! Scouts honor! Tell me that you love me, Junie Moon! Tell me that you love me! I can change for you, Junie Moon, I can change! Oh, you sweet, smoky, scaly, green bombshell, you!

(JUMPER faints backwards onto the STAGE FLOOR, his claws limp and in the air. Kneeling down to help him, JUNIE MOON rubs his belly affectionately)

JUNIE MOON

Jumper? Jumper the Dragon? Are you okay? Speak to me. It's the love of your life, Junie Moon, the most glamorous journalistic newscaster in all the World from W.H.O.P. TV, located in the beautiful downtown burg of Whopperville, U.S.A. Speak to me, Jumper, speak to me!

(JUNIE MOON helps him up as he revives, regaining his faculties, and staggering around)

JUMPER

Never felt better in my life!

(Still tipsy from the effects)

Hey, tootsie, what's happening? Sorry I almost finished you off earlier, but I was just following orders, you know, like a good little soldier! Kiss, kiss, hug, hug, Moon-ski-poo?

(Admiring the REFLECTOR)

Hey, Doc, this looking glass of yours is a great setup! You sure you want to let the Queen here have it? This is quality merchandise! It would be a hot sell at the local bed, bath, and beyond infinity emporium!

QUEEN THIRTEEN

(Irritated by the nonsense)

Silence, ingrate! Out of my way, you treacherous Fairie sizzler! Bring me that mirror! Lay it on me!

JUNIE MOON

(Challenging QUEEN THIRTEEN)

Of all the egotistical nerve! You told me it was my turn to stare into the Vanity-Ego-Reflector! Is it my turn, or isn't it?

(QUEEN THIRTEEN ignors her and turns to CAPTAIN BANDIT, who has been VIDEOGRAPHING the seductive MERMAIDS of MERMAID'S ISLE)

QUEEN THIRTEEN

Aim that video camera at me, Captain Bandit! Don't tarnish your lens by turning it on those tuna titillating tramps!

(CAPTAIN BANDIT obeys)

ETHEL

How rude! Girls, are we going to stand for that kind of treatment? We're far more glamorous than she!

(GERTRUDE and BUFFY look at each other, then at ETHEL, then at QUEEN THIRTEEN, and finally at each other again before they roll their eyes skyward, shrug, and just blow it all off. QUEEN THIRTEEN addresses EVERYONE else by singing "THIRTEENLAND EGO BUSTERS")

QUEEN THIRTEEN

(Strutting about)

It seems to me I have the right to say and do whatever I might / So don't give me a hard old time, I'll zap you silly for it's a crime / No one here is greater than I, for I'm the best and I know why / Thirteenland is nightmares come true, a land where Fairies in Fairie suits turn blue / As they slave away in my Hot House, I'll think up evil deeds to louse up every good intention they have thought up just to get away!

ETHEL, BUFFY, & GERTRUDE

(Sing the CHORUS in three part harmony. The PIRATES sing the bass beats 'Bum, bum, bum, de bum, etc.)

How rude, how rude, that's such an egotistical thing she plans to do. / Those poor sweet Fairies don't stand a chance, her rudeness is supreme, to shatter all those Fairies' hopes and dreams.

JUNIE MOON

(Sings the SECOND VERSE to QUEEN THIRTEEN)

Your ego knows no bounds it's true, but just the same I've got one, too / Because I am a Video Queen, a star of stage and sometimes screen / Don't think you can shove me aside, I'll spar with you and chance my hide / To zapping with your Magic Scepter becoming at once oblivion's specter / For ego is as ego does, so don't blame me you crummy scuzz / I'm videos finest, broadcast from towers, all over this land for hours and hours!

GERTRUDE, BUFFY, & ETHEL

(REPEAT the CHORUS, chastising QUEEN THIRTEEN. The MAGNIFICENT ZEPPELIN CREW dances with the PIRATES while DOCTOR GEORGE conducts the MUSIC and CAPTAIN BANDIT VIDEOGRAPHS the event)

QUEEN THIRTEEN

(Sings the THIRD VERSE to JUNIE MOON, intimidating her with her movements and MAGIC SCEPTER)

Young lady, I don't care if you think egos as yours can squelch me, too / What's more, I plan to make you prisoner, just like those glittering Fairie flitterers / King Jaggar thought to rein all over, until I locked him up forever / Those Fairies, you, and everyone else, will succumb to me for I am jealous / Of anyone who dares be greater, I'll toss you in volcanic craters / Whose red hot flames will make you scream, avenging my Thirteenland dream!

ETHEL, GERTRUDE, BUFFY, & EVERYONE

(They REPEAT the CHORUS, much to QUEEN THIRTEEN'S dismay and disapproval. The SONG comes to a thrilling CLOSE, with EVERYONE SINGING. Stepping forward to address QUEEN THIRTEEN, DOCTOR GEORGE signals SEYMOUR and MAX to bring to her the VANITY-EGO-REFLECTOR)

DOCTOR GEORGE

And now, you're Majesty, Queen Thirteen, I offer to you the gift of my greatest invention, the Vanity-Ego-Reflector! Present her Majesty with our gift, gentlemen!

(THEY place the VANITY-EGO-REFLECTOR)

JUNIE MOON

(Disappointed)

I guess we know who counts around here.

(Dryly to QUEEN THIRTEEN)

Don't let those unsightly bags under your eyes wreck your day.

(Timidly at first, QUEEN THIRTEEN suddenly lunges at the VANITY-EGO-REFLECTOR, nearly knocking it from their grasp. The PULSATING LIGHTS on it SWIRL, SMOKE, SPIRAL, and FLASH as she's given a gut wrenching look at her true self. The VANITY-EGO-REFLECTOR blasts AIR, CONFETTI, and GLITTER at her, just as it did before with JUMPER THE DRAGON)

QUEEN THIRTEEN

(Shrieking, then manic)

Oh, merciful universe! Can my Fairie friends ever forgive me? Will my loving husband, King Jaggar, ever take me back as his wife and Queen? I had no idea I was hurting them so much! I made them suffer because I knew deep down that I was not a true Fairie after all, but a mere mortal like some of you, whom the Fairies adopted when I was a young girl who had run away from home. King Jaggar married me, but I became a Fairie in name only—a noble gesture—but I still didn't belong! Twice in my life I had been rejected, first by my family because my baby sister was cuter than I and therefore more loved—how is it baby sisters are always more loved? And second, by my Fairie friends, whom I was never able to bond with because of my insane jealousy of that same baby sister—whoever she may be!

(SHE breaks loose of the VANITY-EGO-REFLECTOR and stands DOWN CENTER STAGE of it, addressing EVERYONE)

My wings were fake, fake! I couldn't fly and I couldn't glitter like the rest. Naturally, the only thing left for me to do was to take over Jaggar's Isle and enslave everyone with the help of Captain Bandit and his pirate crew!

(The PIRATES glance around, faces covered with guilt)

They only helped me do it because I paid them with the Royal Jewels—pirates will do anything for treasure—but even they can't stand me!

(The PIRATES nod sadly in agreement)

I was a poor little girl, and an evil, wicked creature. So fragile, so unloved, so sorry for hurting anyone—forgive me, cruel world! I'm just a victim of unlikely circumstances! Rescue me, too, someone, won't you?

(QUEEN THIRTEEN faints, drops to the ground CENTER STAGE as JUNIE MOON, JUMPER, MAX, and SEYMOUR rush to her aid. The SPECIAL EFFECTS subside)

JUNIE MOON

Queen Thirteen! Queen Thirteen, dear, please, please, snap out of your trance. Wake up!

JUMPER

Poor, Queenie, I had no idea how much you've suffered. If it's any consolation, I always thought you were an 'interesting' person.

(JUMPER looks around and shrugs as QUEEN THIRTEEN revives. They give her some space)

QUEEN THIRTEEN

Oh, my. Whew, what a relief that was! That was a load off my mind, let me tell you. I feel lighter than air!

(QUEEN THIRTEEN is smiling, breathing deeply as JUNIE MOON sheepishly approaches her)

JUNIE MOON

Miss Thirteen, your Honor, you're Majesty, did that little girl who was your adoring little baby sister, the one who treated you indifferently and without affection.

(She points to her stylish DAME ELIZABETH TAYLOR MOLE)

Did she have a little mole on her cheek like this one, see, like Liz Taylor's?

SEYMOUR

(Blurting out)

You mean your beauty spot is the real thing? It's not a fake? It's a genuine unmistakable mole?

(Disgusted, pointing to the MOLE)

Ugh, a lousy skuzzy mole, and it has hairs in it!

(Ignoring SEYMOUR, QUEEN THIRTEEN and JUNIE MOON recognize one another with a great show of happiness)

QUEEN THIRTEEN

(Repeatedly hugging and kissing)

Merciful moonbeams! You're my long lost baby sister! Oh, what a happy day this is, to be reunited at long last!

JUNIE MOON

You can give up evil forever!

QUEEN THIRTEEN

Yes, my dear, I can forget about all my efforts to terrorize the world and destroy its economy by selling my Thirteenland souvenirs.

(Aside to the AUDIENCE)

I'm sorry if Wall-Street got there first. I'd so wanted to be the first to destroy our fragile global economy!

JUNIE MOON

We can be good friends, just as all sisters should be, without sibling rivalry.

QUEEN THIRTEEN

Now I can set every Fairie creature sweating in my Thirteenland Hot House Trinket Factory, free!

JUNIE MOON

Gosh, if only I had been able to document this wonderful occasion for W.H.O.P. TV!

(CAPTAIN BANDIT goes to JUNIE MOON while still videographing faithfully with her VIDEO CAMERA)

CAPTAIN BANDIT

Don't worry, my salty sea wench, I've got the whole revelation on video for posterity. We are going to be rich when we take this documentary to your W.H.O.P. TV studio! If they won't pay heaps of gold doubloons, jewels, and treasure, I'll hold you for ransom!

(Rushing into CAPTAIN BANDIT'S arms gleefully)

JUNIE MOON

Oh, Captain Bandit, you saved my documentary! I'm yours forever, to love and obey! Take me away on your pirate ship for our honeymoon, posthaste!

(The MERMAIDS, PRINCE, and LADDIE applaud and cheer for CAPTAIN BANDIT and JUNIE MOON. Holding up the VANITY-EGO-REFLECTOR, MAX and SEYMOUR struggle to keep it upright)

CAPTAIN BANDIT

We'll sail the seven seas and make plans to raid the television industry! We'll plunder their products, and make a fortune selling pirated videos!

(SEYMOUR, shocked that he has lost JUNIE MOON, moves away from helping MAX hold up the VANITY-EGO-REFLECTOR)

SEYMOUR

(Sniffling pitifully)

What mischief have we here? Attracted to Captain Bandit? My precious, Junie Moon! I didn't mean to hurt your feelings. I'm not really repulsed by your hairy Liz Taylor mole.

(Alarmed, overwhelmed by jealousy)

This cannot be! You belong to me! He's a pirate and will steal you away on his pirate ship. Your Liz Taylor beauty spot told me so!

MAX

Can a mole raise millions for HIV/AIDS charities, Seymour?

(Struggling with the REFLECTOR)

And thanks for leaving me with holding up the goods that just saved Jaggar's Isle! Hey, Doc, if nobody else wants to take a glance into this contraption of yours, can someone please help me put it away?

DOCTOR GEORGE

Sure, Max. Seymour, help poor Max bring aboard my revolutionary invention!

QUEEN THIRTEEN

I'll miss you, dear Doctor George! You saved our marriage and the Kingdom of Jaggar's Isle! And thanks for reuniting my sister, Junie Moon and I at long last.

DOCTOR GEORGE

Think nothing of it, you were simply the first evil being on our agenda to have their egos exposed by my incredible invention.

QUEEN THIRTEEN

I wish you all well who want to save the world from terrorism, war, destruction, trinket souvenir salesmen, and the resulting economic disaster all that can bring!

DOCTOR GEORGE

Well said, Queen Thirteen, your Elegance!

(To MAX and SEYMOUR)

Please, be careful you two, and gingerly put the Vanity-Ego-Reflector in the crate. Its connection to the dark matter that holds the universe together is highly spiritual. We don't want to damage it as we must continue our journey around the globe, to use its miraculous powers to thwart evil, injustice, fascism, terrorism, bankruptcy, and just plain naughtiness!

(EVERYONE cheers with the VANITY-EGO-REFLECTOR secure, as SEYMOUR again, begins making a fuss)

SEYMOUR

(Grudgingly, feeling sorry for himself)

Humph, women with beauty spots, all they want are pirate captains with scars, eye patches, peg legs, parrots on their shoulders, and Vanity-Ego-Reflectors filled with dark matter, humph.

(Imitating JUNIE MOON)

Oh, please, Mr. Seymour, I'll love you forever but only if you give me my very own personal Vanity-Ego-Reflector! Golly gee! Mirror, mirror, on the wall, who's the biggest patsy of all!? Me, that's who!

MAX

(Annoyed, miffed)

Maybe the man upstairs still loves you, Seymour?

SEYMOUR

(Looking up into the skies)

You mean Him? Hmm, I don't think so—perhaps he loves TV reporters with beauty spots, or pirates with crushes on them. Whoever God is supposed to be, I know he's taking his vengeance out on me right now!

MAX

Seymour, pal, don't you know that it's an insult to the spiritual peace loving peoples of all nations to believe that their higher power, or just say, the universe, is vengeful. Haven't you learned anything from Doctor George?

SEYMOUR

Sure I have. Terrorists have big egos, so what else is new?

MAX

Ego creates the revenge at the hearts of why some individuals become terrorists, but most peoples are content to believe in their creator's forgiveness.

SEYMOUR

Forgiveness for evil people, too? You mean our higher power forgives us when we're bad? Then why do we bother to run around having evil people stare into the Vanity Ego Reflector? Let God do all the work!

MAX

Using the Vanity-Ego-Reflector helps our creator prepare them to enter the hereafter when they can see and accept themselves for who they truly are at the very core of their being?

SEYMOUR

(Not comprehending, but offended)

Huh? What's that you say about the creator? Who is at the core of what? All I was saying, Max, is that women don't need Vanity-Ego-Reflectors when it comes to busting egos! My ego couldn't get more deflated if you sucked it out of my soul with a vacuum cleaner hose! Women…humph, no thanks!

(MAX puts his arm around SEYMOUR'S shoulder, comforting him)

MAX

Cheer up, Seymour, I believe you love your higher power, God and the universe all at the same time, because we're talking about the same thing, our spirituality.

SEYMOUR

(Still confused, thinking carefully)

Hmm, it's all the same thing, eh? Umm, are we talking about the universe, God, our higher power, and Junie Moon?

MAX

Forget about Miss Junie Moon, at least you and I have each other—and Doctor George—and I love you as if you were my own brother! And I don't even have a scuzzy mole on my cheek!

(They hug and rejoin some of the others, sheepishly looking around for approval of their newfound companionship)

SEYMOUR

Thanks, Max, you're the most. You've helped me to forget about those long, long, lonely nights ahead with Doctor George, saving the world from the trauma of evil, destruction, and vengeful terrorism.

(DOCTOR GEORGE rolls his eyes at them, grumbling in order to draw the attention away from their embarrassing situation)

DOCTOR GEORGE

Now that things are looking up, I guess I need to give some of you a ride home. For all who want to come along and experience our thrilling adventures, my Magnificent Zeppelin is yours to command!

ETHEL

You can drop the girls and me off at Mermaid's Isle! We have plenty of sharks there to keep our hands full without running after egotistical terrorists! Sharks are God's little joke on tasty, if not sexy, Mermaids.

PRINCE

(Holding GERTRUDE closely)

You can drop me off there, too!

(To LADDIE, who is holding BUFFY lovingly)

Come along, Laddie and Buffy! Gertrude and I will be in seventh heaven on Mermaid's Isle together! We'll take care of the sharks!

(Agreeing, he hustles BUFFY closer to PRINCE and GERTRUDE)

LADDIE

We're not afraid of them—we'll cut-'em-up and shish kebab them over an open fire! We'd be so happy there! Buffy and Gertrude, are the finest, fishiest--

PRINCE

--Filet-frying-fanciest-females we pirates could ever be lucky enough to bond with!

LADDIE

(Flustered with PRINCE)

I was going to say all that, Prince, you're too quick for me.

PRINCE

Captain Bandit has a saucy new wench who's going to make us all famous with her documentary!

LADDIE

I'm sure wishin' they would be comin' with us instead of going to the U.S.A. to pirate videos. And I'll miss all the pretty Fairies, too.

PRINCE

Yes, to pirate the television industry--a noble cause indeed for our Captain--but Jaggar's Isle, without Thirteenland, will be a much better environment for our Fairie friends, while we enjoy the matrimonial bliss of Mermaid's Isle.

(The PIRATES and MERMAIDS hug and kiss)

DOCTOR GEORGE

Let us hope that Fairie creatures everywhere, especially here on the Isle of Jaggar, will work their magic to help us all to be faithful, loving, caring living beings, dwelling peacefully and harmoniously with one another, without the prejudice, hatred, intolerance, and the injustice that evil demands of oneself.

MAX

Doctor George, that was a mouthful—do you feel okay? It's time we ascended into the skies to continue our mission.

SEYMOUR

Gee whiz, Doctor George, I mean, God bless the universe. I mean, dear universe, please bless God. No, please bless us all, dear higher power.

MAX

Don't forget, all the deity's are one and the same in the universe.

SEYMOUR

Yes, Max, the higher power of the universe helps to heal the universe, while the creator looks on, and helps us with the higher power's approval…and sanctioning….

(Frazzled)

Oh, I give up, I'll never understand the universe, um, the creator!

(He snaps his fingers as a thought comes to him)

I know! We'll call it our higher power, instead! Right, Max, you said so, right?

(EVERYONE ON BOARD is getting anxious to take off and get down to the business of saving the globe from evil. Wearily, MAX sighs and hugs SEYMOUR, pinching his cheek)

MAX

Yes, Seymour, yes, that's a good idea. You amaze me with how sharp you can be sometimes—wow!

(Addressing the AUDIENCE)

Honestly, folks, just substitute your own favorite deity in the proceedings, and forget about the higher universal powers being different from one another. They're all one and the same—well, God help us probably, hopefully, because they're at the core of our being as well!

DOCTOR GEORGE

(Impressed)

Just like dark matter. Honestly, Max, you surprise me, too, with your insight concerning the dark matter within and without the universe.

SEYMOUR

Please, my head is exploding, let's just let the man upstairs figure it all out, and we'll just go about the business of doing whatever it takes to get by in order to save the world.

(MAX plucks a SEQUIN off of the bodice of GERTRUDE, and sticks it on his right cheek a la the LIZ TAYLOR MOLE)

MAX

(Holding SEYMOUR close)

Hush, dear Seymour, hush—all is well with the world, just relax, I'm here for you always, Liz Taylor beauty spot engaged and in place.

JUNIE MOON

Goodbye, Doctor George! My fiancé, Captain Bandit, and I will be returning one day to visit my long lost sister, Blanche, a.k.a. Queen Thirteen, my less-attractive, repugnant much older sibling.

QUEEN THIRTEEN

(Happily)

How marvelous, I'd forgotten I had a mortal name…Blanch. How Tennessee Williams! Goodbye, Doctor George, and thank you for the wonderful gift of restoring me to my earthly human family. Dear Moon-ski-pooh, goodbye, my precious baby sister, and long lost sibling.

(She gives JUNIE MOON a fairwell hug)

I must say, Doctor George, that the gift of bringing my sister and I back together at long last was so life affirming, and—

(Hypnotized by JUNIE MOON'S BEAUTY SPOT she stares astonished at her baby sister's face)

—What's this? I think it just moved! Does it run on batteries? Is that a mole or an insect with antennae crawling around on your face?

JUMPER

(Dryly)

Perhaps it runs on dark matter, too, like the Vanity Ego Reflector.

(QUEEN THIRTEEN, puzzled, shakes her head, then snaps back to attention. She, the FAIRIES, and KING JAGGAR gather around JUNIE MOON to bid their farewells. The FAIRIES, jingling happily, dancing, and prancing, toss CONFETTI and GLITTER, spewing it forth all over the STAGE and into the AUDIENCE. KING JAGGAR also flies about waving his WAND while dispersing GLITTER and CONFETTI)

JUMPER

How sweet, everyone wants to thank you, Doctor, for saving Fairieland. And thanks for curing my bipolar-paranoid-schizophrenia, changing me back again into a happy, green, scaly, fire-breathing-charcoal-broiling-honest-to-goodness dragon. Being mean-spirited and sizzling innocent Fairies just wasn't my style—as part of my nature, maybe, but sans style. Goodbye, Doc, I'll remember you in my flames, er, dreams.

CAPTAIN BANDIT has been lovingly holding onto JUNIE MOON as she now has the VIDEO CAMERA back, videographing the scene as she did in the beginning of the story. He turns to QUEEN THIRTEEN and JUMPER)

CAPTAIN BANDIT

Junie Moon and I will be coming back to visit you on Jaggar's Isle after we successfully ransom our video documentary to the television networks for treasure! You've got a cut in the stakes, too, right doll? Shiver-me-timbers, you ravishing wench, are you my precious, salty, savage Miss Moon, or not?

JUNIE MOON

(Lovingly to CAPTAIN BANDIT)

We'll make pirate history together.

(Addressing SEYMOUR)

Forgive me for leaving you for another man, Seymour, but now that you're a fearless adventuresome hero type, I'm sure you'll be breaking dozens of hearts in much the same way as I broke yours—with the aid of my irresistible Dame Elizabeth Taylor beauty spot!

MAX

(Dryly)

Ah, the old beauty spot angle. But a good idea is a good idea.

SEYMOUR

(Suspicious)

So, she admits it, it was the notorious beauty spot prank after all, or was it?

MAX

(Affectionately)

Forget the 'beauty spot,' Seymour, it just doesn't matter anymore. Say, Seymour, what are you into?

SEYMOUR

Yeah, yeah, Max, you'd be surprised.

(Glancing in JUNIE MOON'S direction)

Miss Moon, my romantic intentions for you are going to have to take a backseat until Max and I graduate from college.

(Confidently hoping to make her jealous)

We've decided to room together while we study to be rocket scientists. We're going to wrap ourselves around each other while doing our studies! Right, Max?

MAX

(Embarrassed, but aroused)

Yes, Seymour, we'll wrap ourselves around our rockets.

(DOCTOR GEORGE grumbles again with embarrassment)

DOCTOR GEORGE

I'm so glad that things are back to normal and everyone's happy! Max, Seymour, to your stations, boys, it's time for us to have liftoff and head out to save the rest of the world from the evils of terrorism, dictators, and unpopular fascist regimes! Goodbye, everyone! Thanks for allowing us to save you and make your life here on Earth a more pleasant experience!

(Lowering his voice and looking around at EVERYONE with businesslike intent)

You'll all be receiving a bill in the mail from my accounting services. What can I tell you—it costs a lot of money to police the world! Just ask the United States Federal Government—of course, we're actually succeeding, and on a much tighter budget!

ETHEL

Dear Doctor George, is there anyone on Earth as good as you? Can there be someone else such as you who can be considered the greatest Doctor on the most Magnificent Zeppelin in existence?

(ETHEL snuggles up to DOCTOR GEORGE)

I think not! Oh, Doctor George, darling, I think we should get better acquainted, don't you?

(She squeezes him)

Will you accept seashells and clams in lieu of American dollars for your services?

DOCTOR GEORGE

(He softens up to her)

We shall see, my dear, we shall see.

(Triumphantly)

Up, up, and away, my Zeppelin Zanies!

(EVERYONE CHEERS and SINGS the SECOND VERSE of "DOCTOR GEORGE'S MAGNIFICENT ZEPPELIN". The CHARACTERS move and DANCE about gaily on the STAGE as CLOUD EFFECTS simulate the MAGNIFICENT ZEPPELIN'S ASCENT. KING JAGGAR FLIES all over THE STAGE again, spewing GLITTER and CONFETTI. All CHARACTERS SING until the END of the SONG as the CLOUD EFFECTS ROLL BY. On the FINAL NOTES the CHARACTERS all wave goodbye to the AUDIENCE. FADE OUT. CURTAIN)

THE END

Properties

Act 1 – Scene 1 – Props

Anchor to Hoist & Drop
Dials and Levers to Pull
Gadgets Emitting Smoke & Steam
Engine Propellers which Spin
Flash Bombs
Pulsating, Flashing Lights
Gang Plank
Large Pickle Barrel with Short Rope tied under the Lid
Plenty of Fresh Dill Pickles in the Barrel
Several Crates near the Pickle Barrel.
Levers & Various Gizmos
Fake Propane Heater Units
Small Handheld Video Camera
Junie Moon's W.H.O.P. TV ID Badge
Junie Moon's unfolding Press Passes and Credit Cards
Spewing, Steaming, & Smoking Pipes
Large Captain's Steering Wheel

Act 1 – Scene 2 – Props

Cannon
Cannon Balls
Crowbar for Prying
Hypnotic Umbrella with Painted Spiral for Spinning
Large Needle & String for Repairing Zeppelin Balloon
Mop, Bucket, & Classic Oil Can
Rag for Dusting
Stork Carrying a Swaddled Baby
Handheld Telescope
Wrench for Fixing Pipes

Act 1 – Scene 3 – Props

Swords for Pirates
Flintlock Guns for Pirates
The Pirate Boat (a cutout prop supported by the three pirates)

Small Torn Gasket which resembles Ethel's Earrings
Ethel's Earrings which resemble the Torn Gasket

Act 1 – Scene 4 – Props

(Same props as before continued)

Act 2 – Scene 1 – Props

Large Bird Cage for Fairies
Glitter & Confetti for Fairies to Distribute
Fairie Wands for Fairies to Wave
Swords for Pirates
Jugs of Wine for Pirates
Marshmallows & Small Fire
Fairies in Butterfly Nets and Cages with King Jaggar
Crate with Computerized, Dark Matter Powered, Vanity-Ego-Reflector
Hypnotic Umbrella with Spiral
Flintlock Guns for Pirates
Sand & Sand Castles for Pirates to Mold
Flash Bomb Firing Scepter for Queen Thirteen

Production Notes

This is a two act musical play, running time estimated to be close to two hours, including a fifteen minute intermission. More important than an elaborate set or special effects are the characters' makeup and costumes.

Doctor George's zeppelin is large, with the cucumber shaped balloon nearly filling the upstage area and drooping toward center stage and up into the flies. Nets and dozens of ropes support the gondola which resembles a Spanish galleon with an upper pilot's deck.

On the deck is the Captain's steering wheel, control levers, flashing lights, and smoke exuding pipes. Offstage fans can whip up a gentle breeze. A few birds can fly by occasionally on invisible wires. In scene two, a stork carrying a swaddled baby from its beak also passes by upstage.

The Mermaid's Isle rolls on from stage left carrying the three Mermaids.

The Isle itself is a rocky coral island with a spot of palm fronds and greenery, nestled on a sandy shell filled beach. Sea shells can decorate the rock, coral, and shell formations.

Jaggar's Isle rolls on from stage left in two sections, a sandy beach for the pirates, and a sacrificial alter which Jumper drags on, coming to a stop on either side of the zeppelin. While on Jaggar's Isle, the pirates can casually lay around on the rocks, drinking wine from jugs while roasting marshmallows over a small fire. Their cutout speedboat can rest at anchor on the shore.

Jumper the Dragon drags a set piece on from stage left. It is a platform supporting jagged rocky posts with Junie Moon lashed between them like Fay Wray in the original "King Kong." He pulls the sacrificial altar with Junie Moon using ropes. Lights can aid in the sacrificial excitement, signaling a thunderstorm with lightning, boosting the ominous event about to begin.

One character, King Jaggar, King of the Fairies, is supposed to fly, but that is not necessary. He can simply dance around with the other Fairies. As exciting as flight can be onstage, it's not necessary.

If controlled flying is possible for the production, it would be preferred for the King. The other Fairies could wear roller skates. A special hooked hand grip for invisible looped end wires for swinging about might be possible, but perhaps too risky for the actors. It would allow more Fairies to fly, however. And all the Fairies should carry confetti and glitter-based pixie dust with them to continuously fling it about at appropriate moments.

A flash bomb goes off stage left through which Queen Thirteen herself enters with the smoke swirling and billowing about. Queen Thirteen is dressed gaudily in black, purple, and red and carries a Magic Scepter, which, when aimed, will flash brightly before a smoke bomb goes off on stage. Her every move can be accented by displaying around her lighting effects, particularly flashing lights.

When Seymour and Max remove the mirror from its crate it is embossed with bright lights—it is a glittering, thrilling sight to everyone onstage. It can spew forth wind, confetti, and light effects. It needs two actors to carry it and hold it up for the actors to stare into the mirror. The frame itself will have to house the effects. It can be like a children's interactive toy, with squeaks and whistles. It's a spectacular effect that is crucial for the audience in accepting it as a life altering experience.

Original Music & Lyrics

"Doctor George's Magnificent Zeppelin"

Music & Lyrics by Grant Sutor Vuille © 2011

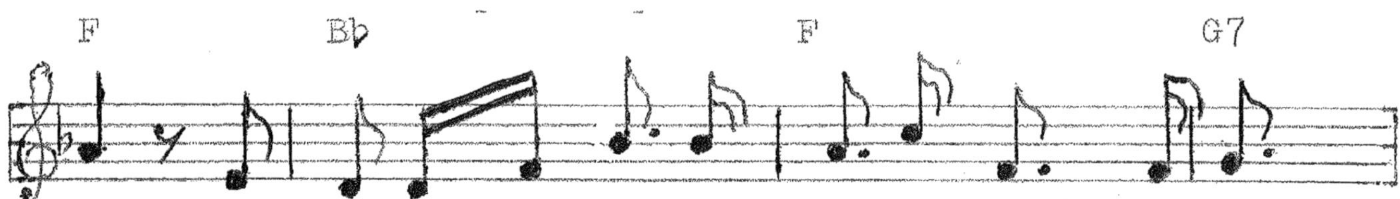

thing. With Seymour and Max right by our sides, we then

can really sing. I'm Dr. George, and this is my magnificent

Zeppelin, so come along. (MAX, SEYMOUR) So come along, (DG)

So come along. We're flying high. (M, S) We're flying high.

(G) So very high. So high, so high. (M, S) So high, so high.

(G) So very high. (M, S) So very high. (G) Up in to the skies!

"The Mermaid's of Mermaid's Isle"

Music & Lyrics by Grant Sutor Vuille © 2011

C
And where do you suppose they were headed, those pir-
F D
ates and that poor girl? To the Isle of Jagger and Qu-
D7 G C
een Thirteen who's anger will surely unfurl. Queen Thirteen has imprisoned, King Jagger and the Fairies, and
F D 3 D7
woe be to those who interfere, a wicked grudge that old
G C
Queen carries. She's a fairy herself but was cast out
3 F D
of fairyland long ago, for making a fuss by consorting
D7 G C
with pirates and becoming the fairies foe. So, please
dear Doctor don't go there, stay and chat with us a while,

F
D
D7
there's trouble there and we're lonely here, be a sport
G
come make us smile — ile — ile — ile — ile!
(ETHEL)
(BUFFY, GERTRUDE) - ON MERMAIDS ISLE, MERMAIDS ISLE, MERMAIDS ISLE!

"Thirteenland Ego Busters"

Music & Lyrics by Grant Sutor Vuille © 2011

(Note by Author) A musical director would be advised to hire musicians who are accustomed to jam session improvising without the need of extensive preparation using predefined arrangements. This will help to develop and enhance a more sophisticated musical score, and aid in finding a suitable, exciting arrangement that will enhance this musical production. The songs can be orchestrated together to create an overture, entr'acte, and exit music.

www.ingramcontent.com/pod-product-compliance
Ingram Content Group UK Ltd.
Pitfield, Milton Keynes, MK11 3LW, UK
UKHW051138260726
13967UKWH00010B/3117